C000231952

Word for Windows:
THE POCKET REFERENCE

Deborah Craig

Osborne **McGraw-Hill**

Berkeley New York St. Louis San Francisco
Auckland Bogotá Hamburg London Madrid
Mexico City Milan Montreal New Delhi Panama City
Paris São Paulo Singapore Sydney
Tokyo Toronto

Osborne **McGraw-Hill**
2600 Tenth Street
Berkeley, California 94710
U.S.A.

For information on translations or book distributors outside of the U.S.A.,
please write to Osborne **McGraw-Hill** at the above address.

Microsoft Word for Windows:
The Pocket Reference

34567890 DOC 9987654

ISBN 0-07-882012-X

For Lisa

CONTENTS

Acknowledgments

Many people made contributions to this book:

- Heidi Steele pitched in with her usual fantastic copy and technical edit, helped me wrestle with beta versions of the software, and met even the most untenable of deadlines.

- Scott Rogers, acquisitions editor, got this project on the road and kept it there, nudging me along whenever I seemed to be flagging.

- Wendy Rinaldi, project editor, also did a superb job under duress, as well as commiserating with me about computer book deadlines in particular and life in general.

- Associate editor Emily Rader graciously checked up on me periodically to see if I was still functioning and to find out whether the next section was ready.

- Sherith Pankratz, editorial assistant, smoothed over many rough edges, most importantly hustling me a check so I didn't miss one of my monthly mortgage installments.

- Micky Galicia, computer designer, not only did an excellent job setting Page Proofs, but made massive last-minute corrections to perfection. This book would not be readable without her.

- Peter Hancik, computer designer, tweaked the book design expertly, saving me from having to cut massive amounts of material in page proofs.

- Dino, Greg Goodman, and Joe Sabella provided many Mondays of dessert, conversation, and music unencumbered by form.

Introduction

This book is a "short and sweet" guide to Word for Windows 6.0. It lets you get straight to the information you need, often without even having to consult the table of contents or index. Whether you're a newcomer or a fairly experienced Word for Windows user, you should be able to flip quickly to the desired topic and get simple step-by-step instructions. In short, you'll learn which keys to press, with a minimum of frills and fuss.

There are two sections in this book. The first, "General Procedures," explains a number of Word for Windows fundamentals. You can read this section for a crash course on Word, or to refresh your memory on certain basics such as how to open files and perform rudimentary editing tasks. Among other things, you'll learn how to start Word; create a new document; issue commands; open, close, and save files; get help in a pinch; and leave Word once you're done. Many of these topics are covered in greater detail later in the book.

If you're familiar with Word for Windows basics, you can jump directly to the second section, "Commands and Features," which makes up the main part of this book. This section covers Word for Windows features in alphabetical order. Numbered lists guide you through the steps necessary to perform each task, and are followed by brief descriptions of the feature, as well as explanations of any of the command's variations or intricacies.

There are a number of simple conventions used throughout this book:

- Commas separate option names and underscores indicate which letter you need to press in menu options.

For example, File, Open means to pull down the File menu and then choose the Open command. Note that you can use mouse or keyboard techniques to choose menu options; for further details, see "Issuing Commands with the Menus" under "General Procedures."

- Keypresses joined by a plus sign are simultaneous. For example, CTRL+B means hold down the CTRL key while pressing B.

- Whenever shortcut techniques are available, they are listed under the "Mouse Shortcut" and "Keyboard Shortcut" headings. *Make sure* not to skip over this material; it teaches you how to work most efficently in Word for Windows.

General Procedures

This section covers basic procedures you will want to
acquaint yourself with if you are new to Word for
Windows, to Windows, or to both. Among other things,
you'll learn such essentials as how to start and leave the
program, how to move around the screen, and how to get
help when you need it. Once you master these
fundamentals, you should be able to comfortably make
use of the alphabetical list of commands and features
that comprises the main part of this book.

How to Use Your Mouse

Knowing how to use a mouse helps you get the most out
of any Windows program, and Word for Windows is no
exception. (If you don't own or don't like to use a mouse,
however, there are usually keyboard alternatives.) If
necessary, read this section to brush up on mouse
techniques; feel free to pass over it if you're already an
accomplished mouse user.

Before you perform any actions with your mouse, you
need to locate the *mouse pointer*, which moves
correspondingly when you move your mouse. Although
the mouse pointer is often shaped like an arrow, it can
take on different shapes depending on where it is
located. For instance, the mouse pointer is shaped like
the letter "I" when positioned over the Word for Windows
editing screen. The mouse pointer indicates where any
actions will take place.

These four basic mouse techniques will almost always
get you where you're going:

- *Pointing* means moving your mouse until the mouse
  pointer is in the desired location on the screen.

- *Clicking* means pointing to the desired location, and
  then pressing down and releasing a mouse button. Typically, this means pressing and releasing the left mouse
  button. On occasion, however, you may need to use the
  right mouse button. (Use the left mouse button unless
  otherwise specified.)

- *Double-clicking* means pointing to the desired location,
  and then clicking the mouse button twice in rapid

succession. (Again, use the left mouse button unless otherwise specified.)

- *Dragging* means pointing to the desired location, holding down the left mouse button, moving the mouse, and then releasing the mouse button.

STARTING WORD FOR WINDOWS

Before you can begin to work in Word for Windows, you need to start it—that is, to bring it up on your computer screen. There are a number of ways of doing this; in particular, you can start Word for Windows either from Windows or from DOS.

Starting from Windows

Even once you're in Windows, there are many ways to start Word for Windows. Try not to be overwhelmed by the wealth of options; most of them are quite simple. (See a Windows text if you're not sure how to start Windows.)

If you're in the Program Manager and the Microsoft Office group window is on the screen, you can start Word for Windows just by double-clicking on its icon, which will most likely have the words "Microsoft Word" beneath it. In a moment, you'll see a mostly blank document screen and you can begin typing and editing your work. (If you see a Tip of the Day, you can clear it from the screen by clicking on OK or pressing ENTER.)

If you can't find the Microsoft Word icon on the Program Manager screen, click on the <u>W</u>indow option at the top of the screen and then type the number to the left of Microsoft Office in the list of program groups that appears (your program group could also have a slightly different name). You may have to select <u>M</u>ore Windows to find the program group name, in which case you just highlight it in the Select Window dialog box and click on OK or press ENTER. (You'll learn more about making menu and dialog box selections in a moment.)

You may find yourself in the Windows File Manager instead of the Program Manager. (You know you're in the File Manager if the words "File Manager" appear at the top of the screen.) If so, you can switch over to the Program Manager by pressing CTRL+ESC, selecting

Program Manager from the Task List, and clicking on the Switch To button. Consult a Windows text or your Windows documentation for more details on these Windows-related topics.

Starting from DOS

To start Word for Windows from DOS, switch to the drive and directory containing the program (most likely C:\WINWORD) and type win winword. If the Word for Windows directory is listed in your DOS search path and you don't have multiple versions of Word for Windows installed, you can enter this command from anywhere in DOS, not just from within the WINWORD directory. (For information about DOS search paths, see your DOS manual.) If you want to load a file as you're starting Word for Windows, simply type its name after the command—as in win winword *filename.*

LEAVING WORD FOR WINDOWS

To ensure that all your work is safely put away, you need to exit Word for Windows whenever you are done with it for the day. Do *not* just turn off your computer while running Word; first leave Word for Windows and then exit Windows itself before turning off your computer.

One way to leave Word for Windows is to choose Exit from the File menu (you can also press ALT+F4). If you've saved all your changes to any open documents, you return directly to Windows. If there are unsaved changes to any open documents, Word for Windows asks if you want to save those changes. Answer Yes to save the changes, No to discard the changes, Cancel to return to the document in question, or Help for more information. (For more details on saving files, see "Saving Files" later in this section, or see SAVE, SAVE ALL, or SAVE AS under "Commands and Features.")

You can also exit Word for Windows by double-clicking on the Control menu box in the upper-left corner of the screen (it looks like a large dash). Make sure to use the dash on the top line of the screen, to the left of the title bar that reads "Microsoft Word." (If you accidentally double-click on the smaller dash directly beneath it, you'll

close the document you're working on but won't exit from
Word for Windows.) Again, you'll be informed if there are
unsaved changes to any open documents.

Once you have left Word for Windows, you can work with
another Windows application, or you can exit to DOS or to
your menu system and turn off your computer for the day.
If you want to return to DOS, make sure you're in the
Windows Program Manager, choose Exit Windows from
the File menu (ALT+F4), and then choose OK or press
ENTER to return to DOS. Alternatively, you can
double-click on the Program Manager's Control menu
box—the dash in the upper-left corner of the screen—and
then choose OK or press ENTER to return to DOS. From here
you can safely turn off your computer.

ENTERING TEXT

Once you've started Word for Windows, you're ready to
enter text. To begin creating a new document, just type
away: Word for Windows automatically opens a blank
document when you start the program. To edit an
existing document—either adding text or making
changes— you'll need to open it first. See "Opening and
Closing Files" later in this section or OPENING FILES
under "Commands and Features."

Like all modern word processors, Word for Windows
includes a feature called *word wrap*. This simply means
that Word knows to proceed to the next line when you
have typed enough words to fill a line with text, and is
smart enough to adjust line breaks later if you go back
and add or delete text. You don't need to (and should not)
press the ENTER key to move to a new line unless you
want to insert blank lines, start a new paragraph, or force
Word to start a new line, no matter the length of the
current line. (You'll usually press ENTER after each line in
an address, for example.)

NAVIGATING IN WORD FOR WINDOWS

Once you've typed some text in Word for Windows, you'll
need to know how to navigate through your document,

either to add or edit text, to move to a location where you
want to make formatting changes, or simply to review
your work up to this point. Note that navigating means
changing your location in the document, and that your
exact location is indicated by the *insertion point*—a
horizontal blinking line that is analogous to the cursor
featured in DOS-based word processors. (Don't confuse
the insertion point with the mouse pointer, which may be
shaped like a capital "I" or like an arrow, depending on
where you are on the screen and what task you're
performing.) Get in the habit of keeping tabs on the
insertion point; this is where text is inserted when you
type; where graphics, tables, and other elements are
placed; where text is pasted (inserted) into your
document—in short, where much of the action happens.

There are two basic means of navigating in Word for
Windows: with the keyboard or with the mouse.

Navigating with the Keyboard

The primary way to move around using the keyboard is to
use the cursor movement keys: HOME, END, PGUP, PGDN,
and the four arrow keys, as described here:

Key	Moves Insertion Point
RIGHT ARROW	One character to the right
LEFT ARROW	One character to the left
UP ARROW	Up one line
DOWN ARROW	Down one line
PGUP	Up one screen
PGDN	Down one screen
HOME	To start of current line
END	To end of current line
ALT+CTRL+PGUP	To beginning of previous page
ALT+CTRL+PGDN	To beginning of next page
CTRL+RIGHT ARROW	One word to right
CTRL+LEFT ARROW	One word to left
CTRL+PGUP	To first character in current screen
CTRL+PGDN	To last character in current screen
CTRL+HOME	To top of document

Key	Moves Insertion Point
CTRL+END	To bottom of document
CTRL+UP ARROW	Up one paragraph*
CTRL+DOWN ARROW	Down one paragraph*

* Word considers a paragraph to be any amount of text—whether a single
  character or many sentences—followed by a paragraph mark (you introduce
  a paragraph mark by pressing ENTER).

You can also move around with the Edit, Go To command
(F5), which lets you travel to a more specific location in
the current document. You can use Go To to move to a
particular page, a footnote, an annotation, or a specific
line of text, among other things. For details, see GO TO
under "Commands and Features." Go To can be a fast and
accurate way of navigating in longer documents,
especially if you have a good idea of your desired
destination.

Here's one final way of moving around in your document
with the keyboard: Word remembers the last three places
where you edited or typed text, and you can return to
those locations by pressing SHIFT+F5. This feature is
invaluable when you are working in several distant areas
of a long document, or when you accidentally press a
cursor movement key and want to return to your previous
location.

Navigating with the Mouse

With the mouse, you can go to a different place in your
document simply by moving the mouse pointer and
clicking where you want to place the insertion point.
Make sure the mouse pointer looks like an uppercase "I"
when you click (this is called the *I-beam pointer*); if it
looks like an arrow, you'll wind up selecting text rather
than just moving the insertion point.

If you want to move to an area that is not currently
visible on the screen, first use the vertical scroll bar at
the right side of the screen to bring it into view. (This
changes your view of the document but does *not* move
the insertion point.) Click on the scroll arrows at the top
and bottom of the scroll bar to move up or down one line
at a time. The double arrows available near the bottom of
the scroll bar in Page Layout view and Print Preview let
you move up and down one page at a time. Drag the

scroll box up or down to move through your document in larger increments. Drag the box to the bottom of the scroll bar to move to the bottom of your document, for example. You can also click on the scroll bar itself to move up (click above the scroll box) or down (click below the scroll box) one screenful at a time. When you've scrolled to the desired location, just click the left mouse button to relocate the insertion point.

EDITING TEXT

You can use cursor movement keys, the mouse, or both to get to the area of the document you want to edit. Once you're there, you have a number of options for editing your text. This section just discusses how to add and delete text. For details on making more specific text formatting changes such as boldfacing, selecting different fonts, and so on, consult the relevant sections in the "Commands and Features" portion of this book. To customize certain aspects of editing in Word for Windows, see "Edit" under OPTIONS.

Adding Text

To add text to your document, simply move the insertion point to the desired location and begin to type. Any subsequent text will be pushed to the right and down to compensate. Because of the word wrap feature, Word for Windows automatically adjusts line breaks.

If you want to type over existing text instead of inserting new text, you can switch to overtype mode by pressing the INS key or double-clicking on the OVR indicator in the lower-right corner of your screen. (The letters "OVR" will turn black.) To turn off overtype mode, press INS or double-click on OVR again. (See OVERTYPE MODE.)

Deleting Text

There are a number of ways of deleting text in Word for Windows, as outlined here:

Key	Action
DEL	Deletes a single character to the right of the insertion point

Key	Action
BACKSPACE	Deletes a single character to the left of the insertion point
CTRL+DEL	Deletes a single word to the right of the insertion point*
CTRL+BACKSPACE	Deletes a single word to the left of the insertion point*
CTRL+Z or ALT+BACKSPACE	Reverses the previous action; if your last action was to type some text, CTRL+Z or ALT+BACKSPACE deletes that text

* If the insertion point is in the middle of a word, deletes the portion of the word to the left or right of the insertion point, respectively.

You can also delete selected text: First you select the text to be deleted and then you press DEL or BACKSPACE. This method is more efficient if you're deleting more than just a little bit of text. You'll learn how to select text in a moment. (Some word processing programs refer to this process as "blocking" text.) Note that you can delete and add text at the same time by selecting the text to be deleted and then typing the text you want to replace it with.

If you want to delete text from one location and place it in another—as opposed to deleting it permanently—refer to CUT AND PASTE and SPIKE under "Commands and Features."

SELECTING TEXT

In Word, as in many other word processors, you can select a block of text and then perform actions that affect the entire block. (Selected text is shown in reverse video, generally with white text on a black background.) For example, you can select a block of text and then delete the entire block at once. It is also possible to select text and then format it in a variety of ways, move it to a different location, and more. You can select any amount of text—from a single character to your entire document—and you can select text with either the keyboard or the mouse.

"Deselecting" selected text just involves clicking the left mouse button anywhere within the editing screen, or pressing any of the cursor movement keys. (The ESC key does not work in this context.)

Selecting Text with the Keyboard

Most keyboard methods of selecting text involve the SHIFT key, as you can see here:

Key	Action
SHIFT+RIGHT ARROW	Selects one character to the right
SHIFT+LEFT ARROW	Selects one character to the left
SHIFT+UP ARROW	Selects one line up
SHIFT+DOWN ARROW	Selects one line down
SHIFT+PGUP	Selects up one screen
SHIFT+PGDN	Selects down one screen
SHIFT+HOME	Selects to start of line
SHIFT+END	Selects to end of line
CTRL+SHIFT+RIGHT ARROW	Select to end of word
CTRL+SHIFT+LEFT ARROW	Selects to beginning of word
CTRL+SHIFT+UP ARROW	Selects to beginning of paragraph
CTRL+SHIFT+DOWN ARROW	Selects to end of paragraph
CTRL+SHIFT+PGUP	Selects from insertion point to first character in current screen
CTRL+SHIFT+PGDN	Selects from insertion point to last character in current screen
CTRL+SHIFT+HOME	Selects to beginning of document
CTRL+SHIFT+END	Selects to end of document
CTRL+5 (numeric keypad) or CTRL+A	Selects entire document
ALT+5 (numeric keypad)	Selects table (NUM LOCK must be off and insertion point must be inside table)
CTRL+SHIFT+F8	Selects columns of text when used in combination with arrow keys or mouse (press ESC, click the left mouse button, or press CTRL+SHIFT+F8 again to return to normal selection mode)

You can also select text by pressing F8 or double-clicking on the letters "EXT" at the bottom of the screen to get into extend mode (the EXT indicator will darken). Then do one of the following:

- Press F8 several times to select the desired amount of text. This method first selects a word, then a sentence, then a paragraph, then a section, and finally the entire document (if it consists of more than one section). Press SHIFT+F8 to reverse this process.

- Use the cursor movement keys to select text. (You needn't press SHIFT with the cursor movement keys in this context.)

- Press any character to extend the selection to the next instance of that character. For example, pressing (period) generally extends the selection to the end of the current sentence.

- Use the Find or Go To features to select through to the designated location. See FINDING TEXT, FORMATTING, AND SPECIAL CHARACTERS and GO TO under "Commands and Features."

When you're done selecting text, press ESC or double-click on the EXT indicator to turn off extend mode so that pressing the cursor movement keys or using any of the other techniques described here no longer selects text automatically.

Selecting Text with the Mouse

There are a variety of ways of selecting text with a mouse. You can select any amount of text by dragging with the mouse. To do so, simply place the insertion point where you want the selection to begin, hold down the left mouse button, and drag in any direction until you've selected the desired block of text. (Hold down ALT while you drag to select a perfectly rectangular block of text.) You can also select any amount of text by placing the insertion point where you want the selection to begin, holding down SHIFT, and then clicking where you want the selection to end. This method tends to be more accurate than dragging (where it's easy to overshoot your mark), and is often easier when you're selecting large blocks of text. Word for Windows' Automatic Word Selection feature ensures that only entire words are selected when you select multiple words using either of these techniques. (You can turn this feature off if you like; see "Edit" under OPTIONS.)

In addition, there are mouse techniques for selecting discrete portions of text such as words, sentences, and paragraphs. For example, you can select a single word of text by double-clicking on it, you can select a sentence by holding down the CTRL key and clicking anywhere within the sentence, and you can triple-click to select the current paragraph.

You can select blocks of text by moving the mouse pointer into the *selection bar* at the left edge of the document screen and performing the actions described next. (The selection bar is not marked off, but you know you're there when the mouse pointer changes from an I-beam into an arrow pointing to the right.)

- You can select a line of text by moving the mouse pointer into the selection bar to the left of that line and clicking.

- You can select multiple lines by dragging the mouse pointer through the selection bar to the left of those lines.

- You can select a paragraph by double-clicking to its left in the selection bar.

- You can select several paragraphs by double-clicking the selection bar and then dragging (make sure to keep the mouse button held down after the second click).

- You can select the entire document by triple-clicking or by holding down CTRL while clicking anywhere in the selection bar.

There are also a few selection techniques specific to tables; you'll learn about these in the TABLES section under "Commands and Features."

ISSUING COMMANDS

One of Word for Windows' assets is that it provides a variety of ways of issuing commands. You can use the menus and, in some cases, you can use shortcut key combinations. In addition, Word for Windows offers a full complement of mouse shortcuts—primarily in the form of buttons located in toolbars across the top of the screen.

Issuing Commands with the Menus

You gain access to the Word for Windows menu system via the menu bar at the top of the screen. This menu bar includes the options File, Edit, View, Insert, Format,

Tools, Table, Window, and Help. Selecting any one of these options pulls down a corresponding menu with a further list of options.

You can display a menu with either the keyboard or the mouse. With the keyboard, press the ALT key in combination with the underlined letter in the menu bar option name. For example, to pull down the File menu, press ALT+F. Once the menu appears, you can choose options by typing the underlined letter (mnemonic) in the option name. For example, to choose the Save option in the File menu, just type S. You can also use the UP ARROW or DOWN ARROW key to highlight a menu option, and then press ENTER to select it. As you highlight menu options in this way, a brief command description appears in the lower-left corner of the screen.

If you're using a mouse, you can pull down a menu by clicking on its name with the left mouse button. When a menu is displayed, you select an option by clicking on it.

There are several menu conventions that you should know about:

- Option names followed by ellipses (...) lead to dialog boxes requesting further information.

- Menu options that are grayed (dimmed) are not available in the current context. As one example, most of the options on the Table menu are not available unless you've inserted a table into your document and the insertion point is positioned within it.

- Menu options preceded by a check mark are currently selected; selecting them again turns off the feature. (The exception is that, in the View menu, the Normal, Outline, Page Layout, and Master Document options have a bullet to their left when selected—since only one of these four options can be selected at a time.)

- If a menu option has a key or key combination listed to its right, you can issue that command by pressing that *keyboard shortcut*, without first accessing the menu system. (For instance, you can issue the File, Save command by pressing CTRL+S.) You'll learn more about these shortcut keys in a moment.

Word for Windows enables you to customize the contents and layout of the menu system; see CUSTOMIZE in "Commands and Features" for details.

Shortcut Menus

Word for Windows 6.0 offers *shortcut menus,* a new
feature that lets you access relevant commands more
quickly in certain cases. You display shortcut menus by
placing the mouse pointer on an item and clicking the
right mouse button. For example, clicking the right
mouse button while the mouse pointer is within some
text displays a menu with the options Cut, Copy, Paste,
Font, Paragraph, and Bullets and Numbering. And if you
click the right mouse button anywhere on the toolbars at
the top of the screen, you'll see a menu listing many of
the available toolbars, plus the choices Toolbars and
Customize. You can also right-click on tables or graphics
to display shortcut menus of pertinent commands. In
other words, clicking on certain items with the right
mouse button takes you directly to a "context-sensitive"
menu of options related to the currently selected object or
the items at hand.

Contending with Dialog Boxes

Often when you issue a command, Word for Windows
does not execute an action immediately, but instead
displays a dialog box to request additional information.
Dialog boxes may contain some unfamiliar elements, as
you can see in the Font dialog box shown here (choosing
Format, Font opens this dialog box).

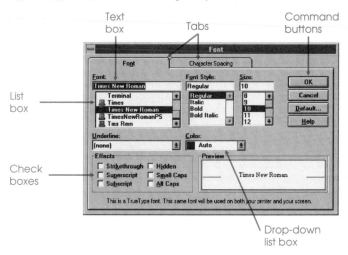

- *Text boxes* are simply boxes—such as the one directly underneath Font—in which you can enter and edit text much as you do within your documents.

- *List boxes* contain lists of options or items (such as the list of font names underneath the Font text box) from which you can choose. They may include scroll bars if there are too many items to fit in the list box at once. Often, as in this case, there are associated text boxes and list boxes (sometimes called *combo boxes*); when you make a selection in the list box, it appears in the associated text box automatically.

- *Drop-down list boxes* are much like list boxes, but only display one item at a time by default. To display the entire list of items, click on the downward pointing arrow at the right end of the list box. (In the dialog box shown here, both Underline and Color are drop-down list boxes.)

- *Check boxes* are square boxes, such as Superscript and All Caps under Effects, that contain an "x" if selected and are blank if not selected.

- *Option buttons* (or *radio buttons*) are round buttons that are filled in if selected, and empty if not; unlike most check boxes, radio buttons that are grouped together always list mutually exclusive options, only one of which can be selected at once. (There are no option buttons in the current dialog box.)

- *Tabs* look like the tabs on a folder and enable you to travel from one "page" of the dialog box to another. For example, the Font dialog box contains the two tabs, Font and Character Spacing.

- *Command buttons* are rectangular buttons (such as OK and Cancel) that you click on to perform an action, or in certain cases to proceed to another dialog box. (Such command buttons are followed by ellipses. OK and Cancel are the two crucial command buttons: You use Cancel to leave a dialog box without putting any changes into place, and OK to leave a dialog box and have the specified changes take effect.

Maneuvering in dialog boxes is exceedingly easy if you're using a mouse: You just click to select things. You click to move into text boxes in order to type; you click to select items in list boxes or drop-down list boxes; you click to select check boxes, and again to deselect them; you click on the downward pointing arrow when you want to see (or close) a drop-down list box; you click to switch between tabs; and you click to select option buttons or command buttons.

If you're using a keyboard, however, there are a few more tricks of the trade. One of the first things to remember is that you must press ALT in combination with an underlined letter to select an item. For example, you must press ALT+S to move to the Size text box in the Font dialog box. Once you're there, you can type in a new point size or you can press the arrow keys to move through the selections in the list box, which are automatically reflected in the text box. For drop-down list boxes, pressing ALT plus the appropriate underlined letter actually pulls down the list box; use the arrow keys to move through the selections, and press ESC to close the list and select the highlighted item. For check boxes, pressing ALT plus the underlined letter selects the check box, or deselects it if it's already selected.

The other main keyboard technique for moving through dialog boxes is the TAB key, which moves you from one item to the next in the dialog box (SHIFT+TAB does the same thing, but moving in the opposite direction). In certain cases—check boxes and command buttons, for example—pressing TAB moves you to the desired location but does not actually make a selection. With check boxes, you can then select (or deselect) them by pressing the SPACEBAR; with command buttons, you can press ENTER once the button is highlighted. Only press ENTER once you've made all the desired selections in the dialog box, since doing so is tantamount to selecting the currently highlighted command button, which is usually OK.

Issuing Commands with Keyboard Shortcuts

A number of common commands have shortcut keys or key combinations that you can use to issue the command without going through the menu system. Note that you can also add, change, and delete keyboard shortcuts, as discussed under CUSTOMIZE in the "Commands and Features" section.

Here's a selective list of common keyboard shortcuts that make use of the function keys at the top or left side of your keyboard. Additional shortcuts may be listed where relevant in the "Commands and Features" section of this book.

Key	Description	Menu Equivalent
F1	Displays help on the current topic	
CTRL+F2	Opens or closes Print Preview display	File, Print Preview
ALT+SHIFT+F2 or SHIFT+F12	Saves the current document with the same name	File, Save
ALT+CTRL+F2 or CTRL+F12	Opens an existing document	File, Open
SHIFT+F3	Changes capitalization of selected text	Format, Change Case
F4	Repeats previous command	Edit, Repeat
ALT+F4	Exits from Word for Windows	File, Exit
CTRL+F4	Closes the active document	File, Close
SHIFT+F4	Repeats last Go To or Find command	
F5	Moves insertion point to the specified location	Edit, Go To
SHIFT+F5	Returns you to a previous position	
F7	Checks spelling of document or selected text	Tools, Spelling
SHIFT+F7	Hunts for synonyms of current word	Tools, Thesaurus
F10	Activates menu bar	ALT
F12	Saves the current document with a new name	File, Save As
CTRL+SHIFT+F12	Prints the current document	File, Print

Here's a selective list of the keyboard shortcuts that do not make use of the function keys. Again, additional shortcuts may be listed where relevant in the "Commands and Features" section of this book.

Key	Description
CTRL+SPACEBAR	Removes formatting from selected text
CTRL+1	Introduces single spacing
CTRL+2	Introduces double spacing
CTRL+A	Selects the entire document
CTRL+B	Turns boldfacing on or off for selected text
CTRL+C	Copies the selected text to the Clipboard
CTRL+D	Displays the font dialog box
CTRL+E	Centers current paragraph
CTRL+F	Displays the Find dialog box
CTRL+G	Displays the Go To dialog box
CTRL+H	Displays the Replace dialog box
CTRL+I	Turns italic on or off for selected text
CTRL+J	Justifies current paragraph
CTRL+L	Left-aligns current paragraph
CTRL+M	Indents paragraph one tab stop
CTRL+SHIFT+M	Unindents paragraph one tab stop
CTRL+SHIFT+N	Applies Normal style
CTRL+N	Opens new file using Normal template
CTRL+O	Displays the Open dialog box
CTRL+P	Displays the Print dialog box
CTRL+Q	Removes paragraph formatting
CTRL+R	Right-aligns current paragraph
CTRL+S	Saves the current document with the same name
CTRL+T	Creates a hanging indent
CTRL+SHIFT+T	Removes hanging indent
CTRL+U	Turns underlining on or off for selected text
CTRL+V	Pastes (inserts) text from Clipboard
CTRL+X	Removes (cuts) selected text and places it on Clipboard
CTRL+Y	Repeats the previous command
CTRL+Z or ALT+BACKSPACE	Undoes the previous action, if possible

Issuing Commands with Mouse Shortcuts

For your convenience, Word for Windows provides a large selection of mouse shortcuts for issuing commands. This section briefly describes the buttons on the Standard toolbar just below the title bar, and on the Formatting toolbar right below that. There are a number of other available toolbars, most of which you can display by choosing Toolbars from the View menu. In addition, there are some specialized toolbars for outlining, working with macros, creating headers and footers, working with master documents, and more. These toolbars, as well as some additional mouse shortcuts, are introduced where relevant in the "Commands and Features" section of this book. Word for Windows also enables you to customize the toolbars, as described under CUSTOMIZE.

Note that positioning the mouse pointer over a toolbar button displays the button's name, as well as a brief description of that button in the lower-left corner of the screen, assuming that the button is available in the current context. In addition, when you select toolbar buttons that are toggles (they turn a feature both on and off), they look as though they've been pressed in when the feature is turned on. Finally, in certain cases toolbars will be inserted into the middle of your editing screen instead of above or below it. You can drag these toolbars by their title bars to move them out of the way, and you can even drag them outside of the editing area to place them at the edge of your screen. (See TOOLBARS.)

These buttons are available on the Standard toolbar:

Button	Description	Menu Equivalent
	Creates a new document	File, New
	Opens an existing document	File, Open
	Saves the active document	File, Save
	Prints all pages of current document	File, Print, OK
	Switches to Print Preview	File, Print Preview
	Spell checks the active document	Tools, Spelling
	Cuts the selected material, placing it in the Clipboard	Edit, Cut

Button	Description	Menu Equivalent
	Copies the selected material, placing it in the Clipboard	Edit, Copy
	Pastes Clipboard contents into document at insertion point	Edit, Paste
	Copies formatting of selected text to location you indicate	
	Undoes previous action, if possible (you can undo multiple actions)	Edit, Undo
	Reverses previous undo, if possible (you can redo multiple actions)	Edit, Redo
	Formats document automatically	Format, AutoFormat
	Inserts or creates AutoText entry	Edit, AutoText
	Inserts table of a specified number of rows and columns	Table, Insert Table
	Opens Excel worksheet	Insert, Object, Microsoft Excel Worksheet
	Formats current document section into specified number of columns	Format, Columns
	Displays or hides the Drawing toolbar	View, Toolbars, Drawing
	Starts Microsoft Graph	Insert, Object, Microsoft Graph
	Displays or hides all special nonprinting characters such as tabs, spaces, and paragraph marks	Tools, Options, View, All
100%	Enables you to zoom or unzoom the display	View, Zoom
	Enables you to click on items and display context- specific help information	View, Zoom

These buttons are available on the Formatting toolbar:

Button	Description
Normal	Lets you select a style
Times New Roman	Lets you select a font

Button	Description
`10`	Lets you select a point size
B	Boldfaces or removes boldfacing from selected text
I	Italicizes or removes italics from selected text
U	Underlines or removes underlining from selected text
	Left-aligns current paragraph or selected paragraphs
	Centers current paragraph or selected paragraphs
	Right-aligns current paragraph or selected paragraphs
	Justifies current paragraph or selected paragraphs
	Formats the selected paragraphs as a numbered list
	Formats the selected paragraphs as a bulleted list
	Shifts the selected paragraphs one tab stop to the left
	Shifts the selected paragraphs one tab stop to the right
	Displays or hides the Borders toolbar

Canceling Commands

There will be times when you decide in midstream not to execute a command after all. You can pursue a number of strategies for backing out of commands, depending on what you're doing and how far you've gotten.

If you decide to leave a menu without issuing a command, you can press the ESC key twice to close the menu and return to the document screen (pressing ESC once closes the menu but leaves you on the menu bar). If you prefer using the mouse, just click anywhere outside the displayed menu to both close the menu and return to the editing screen.

If you're in a dialog box and decide not to continue, either click on Cancel or press ESC to close the dialog box. If you don't see a Cancel button, you can click on Close or double-click on the Control menu box (it looks like a dash) in the upper-left corner of the dialog box.

If you change your mind after typing text or issuing a command, you can in some cases reverse the change with Edit, Undo (CTRL+Z). You can even select this command repeatedly to undo your last several changes. If you change your mind about something that you've undone, you can reverse the undo operation with the Redo command on the Edit menu. (This command is only available if you've undone an action.) The Undo and Redo buttons on the Standard toolbar duplicate the Undo and Redo commands. However, they display lists of the actions that you can undo or redo, and also permit you to undo or redo multiple actions at once. For details, see UNDO and REDO in the "Commands and Features" section of this book.

MANAGING YOUR DOCUMENTS

To do any useful work in Word for Windows, you need to learn how to manage your documents. In particular, you must know how to open existing documents so you can work with them again, and how to save documents so you can come back to them later. It's less necessary, but handy nonetheless, to know at least a bit about how to work with several documents at once.

Opening and Closing Files

When you first start Word for Windows, you'll see a blank document screen—a new, empty document. (If you see a tip instead, clear it from the screen by clicking on OK.) If you want to create a new document, just start typing. However, if you have to work on a document you created earlier, or if you need to review a file that someone else has bestowed upon you, you must use the File, Open command (CTRL+O) to display it on the screen. (You can also use the Open button on the Standard toolbar, as described earlier.) Once you issue this command, you can type in the name of the desired file (make sure the correct directory is selected) or select it from the list of file names that is displayed. If necessary, first choose the drive and directory in which the file is stored.

When you're done working with a file, you should close it with the File, Close command. Keep in mind, however, that you needn't close one file just because you want to open another. In fact, you can open as many files at a time as your computer's memory permits. For more details, see OPENING FILES and CLOSING FILES under "Commands and Features."

Saving Files

When you're creating a new document or modifying an existing document, your words are temporarily stored in the computer's memory, but that memory is like a slate that is wiped clean each time you turn off your computer. If you want your new document—or your newly changed document—to be stored more permanently so you can come back to it later, you need to save it to disk, either your hard disk or a floppy.

To save a document to your disk for the first time, issue the File, Save As command. This opens the Save As dialog box. Under File Name, type a file name of up to eight characters and then click on OK or press ENTER. (Word for Windows automatically assigns the three-letter extension .DOC. Although you can enter a different extension if you like, using the default makes it easier to find and work with your files in the future.) File names can include numbers, letters, and certain special characters such as %, –, #, and @, but cannot include spaces. Files are automatically saved on the current drive and directory; however, you can also save them on a drive and/or directory other than the default by changing the Directories and Drives settings in the Save As dialog box. For example, you can select drive A or B to save your file on a floppy disk for backup purposes. (See DIRECTORIES.)

Once you've named and saved a document initially, you can save any changes to it just by issuing the File, Save command or clicking on the Save button. This automatically overwrites the old copy of the file with the new version. If instead you want to keep both the old and the new versions, you can save the revised file under a new name by using the File, Save As command.

You should save your document regularly as you work. If you lose power, someone kicks your power cord, or your computer dies an untimely death, you don't want to have to manually reconstruct long hours of hard work. The best insurance is to save regularly to both your hard disk and a floppy. That way you have an extra copy of your document on a floppy if your hard disk bites the dust, and you have a current version of the file on your hard disk in case your floppy becomes corrupted. To be completely safe, have two copies on floppy disk, and store one disk off site—preferably in a safety deposit box or some other safe haven.

You can also use the File, Save All command if you want to save changes you've made to several currently open files. For more details on the various save commands, see SAVE, SAVE ALL, and SAVE AS under "Commands and Features." In addition, note that you can to a certain degree control when and how Word saves your work. (As just one example, you can tell Word to save your work automatically at a stipulated interval.) For further information, see "Save" under OPTIONS.

Working with Multiple Documents

You can open many documents at once in Word for Windows, each in its own separate document window. To open more than one document, just use the File, Open command to retrieve additional documents, without closing the documents that you have already opened. Don't be put off when the original document disappears from the screen: It's still there; it has just been obscured by the new document you opened.

There is a difference between an *open* document and an *active* document, which is the one you're working on at the moment. You can have many documents open at once, but only one of them can be active. If you have several documents open at a time, it's easy to switch between them—that is, to change which one is the active document. An easy way to do so (one that also lets you survey a list of the currently open documents) is to pull down the Window menu and choose from the list of files that appears. If you want to see all open windows at once, choose Arrange All from the Window menu. (See WINDOWS in the "Commands and Features" section of this book for more details.)

When you're done working with open files, you can close
them one by one; the File, Close command you learned
about a moment ago closes the active document.
However, you can also close all open documents at once
by holding down the SHIFT key while opening the File
menu, and then choosing Close All. If you issue the Close
or Close All command and there are unsaved changes to
one or more of your documents, Word gives you the
opportunity to save those changes.

THE DIFFERENT VIEWS

One of Word for Windows' assets is that it offers a
number of different ways of viewing your work. Most of
the time you will probably work in *Normal view*, which is
straightforward, fast, and displays more text at a time
than some of the other views. However, at times you may
want to switch to *Page Layout view*—a much closer
approximation of the printed page. In Page Layout view
you can see columns side by side, page numbers,
footnotes on the page, and more. Word also offers a Print
Preview mode to help you see what your documents will
look like when printed. In addition, Word offers an
Outline view. This view provides a number of outlining
features that, among other things, enable you to
"collapse" your document to get an overview, and easily
reorganize your outline. For further information, consult
OUTLINING under "Commands and Features." Finally, you
can work in *Master Document view*, which is like an
outline view for working with master documents. (Master
documents enable you to combine subdocuments so that
you can more easily work with longer documents; see
MASTER DOCUMENTS.)

You can switch views via the View menu, and you can
also use the three view buttons to the left of the
horizontal scroll bar to switch to Normal view (the left
button), Page Layout view (the middle button), and
Outline view (the right button). To open a Print Preview
screen, choose File, Print Preview.

Besides altering the way your document is displayed, you
can change how much of it is displayed. Choose Full
Screen from the View menu to conceal everything but the
editing screen. You can click on the Full icon that appears

in the lower-right corner of the screen (or press ESC) to bring the menu bars and other screen elements back into view. (Note that menus, shortcut menus, and shortcut keys are available, even in full screen view.) You can also use the View menu's Zoom option (or the Zoom Control box on the Standard toolbar) to enlarge or reduce your text—seeing more of it in less detail or less of it in greater detail. Both the Full Screen and the Zoom feature work in any of the views.

WHEN YOU NEED HELP

Help is the single feature most likely to make you self-sufficient in Word for Windows. If you have a memory lapse, or need a quick description of how to accomplish something you've never tried before, Word's help system should be one of the first places you go.

If you are simply typing text and are not in the process of issuing a command, pressing F1 (or choosing Help, Contents) brings up the help system's table of contents screen. (You can return to this screen at any time just by choosing the Contents button in the upper-left corner of the help screen.) From here, among other things, you can click on Using Word to display a list of general topics, and you can click on Examples and Demos to gain access to detailed step-by-step demonstrations of how to perform specified tasks.

Another invaluable area of the help system is the Search dialog box, which you can use to hunt for particular topics. (Either choose Help, Search for Help on; double-click on the Help button at the right end of the Standard toolbar; or, if you're already in the help system, click on the Search button in the upper-left corner of the screen.) Just type a topic, or scroll to a topic, and then click on the Show Topics button to display a list of available help screens at the bottom of the dialog box. Then select the desired topic and click on the Go To button to open the desired help screen. You can also survey an alphabetical list of topics by choosing Index from the Help menu, or by clicking on the Index button once you're in the help system. Click on the letters at the top of the screen to go to the desired location in the list, and click on topics to go to relevant help screens.

Essential to the help system are *jumps*: underlined terms
or phrases that are displayed in a contrasting shade or
color (probably in green if you have a color monitor).
When you point to a jump, the mouse pointer changes
into a hand with an extended index finger. Jumps
indicate that there is additional information on the
subject at hand. Clicking on a jump with a dotted
underline displays a pop-up window with an explanation of
the term or phrase in question. Clicking on a jump with a
solid underline leads to a related help screen.

If you are in the process of issuing a command, pressing
F1 brings up *context-sensitive help*—that is, help related
to the command or topic in question. For example, if you
press F1 from within the Print dialog box, Word for
Windows displays a help screen about the Print
command. Context-sensitive help is like an express train
that takes you directly to the help information you need.
In Word for Windows 6.0, you can get context-sensitive
help via the Help button at the far right end of the
Standard toolbar. When you click on this button, the
mouse pointer changes into an arrow with a question
mark attached. At this point, you can click on screen
elements, choose toolbar buttons, or select menu
commands to obtain context-sensitive help on those
topics. You can even click on text to see what formatting
has been applied to it. If necessary, Press ESC or click on
this Help button again to return to normal editing mode.

Word for Windows' help system includes a wealth of
other features that are beyond the scope of this book.
Among other things, it provides special assistance for
former WordPerfect users, lets you retrace your steps in
the help system with the History command button, and
enables you to annotate help topics, adding your own
notes and comments to them. If you need further
assistance, or are simply curious about additional aspects
of the help system, choose Help, How to Use Help (or
press F1) from within the help system.

To leave the help system, choose File, Exit, or double-
click on the Control menu icon (the dash) in the upper-left
corner of the help screen. If a How To help screen is still
displayed, you can clear it from your screen by clicking on
its Close button.

Commands and Features

The main body of this book consists of the following
alphabetical list of commands and features. For each
feature or command, you learn the appropriate menu
selections, keyboard shortcuts where they exist, and
corresponding toolbar button or mouse techniques if
applicable. You'll also learn about when and why you'd
use the feature in question. If you can't find what you
want in this alphabetical listing, the index at the end of the
book should help you track down the information you need.

ALIGNMENT

1. Place the insertion point in the paragraph to be aligned
   or select at least some portion of all paragraphs to be
   aligned.
2. Choose Format, Paragraph.
3. If necessary, choose the Indents and Spacing tab.
4. Pull down the Alignment drop-down list box.
5. Select Left, Centered, Right, or Justified.
6. Click on OK or press ENTER.

Keyboard Shortcuts:

CTRL+L   Left-aligns selected paragraph(s)
CTRL+E   Centers selected paragraph(s)
CTRL+R   Right-aligns selected paragraph(s)
CTRL+J   Justifies selected paragraph(s)

Mouse Shortcuts:

    Left-aligns selected paragraph(s)

    Centers selected paragraph(s)

    Right-aligns selected paragraph(s)

    Justifies selected paragraph(s)

Determines how paragraph text is arranged between the
left and right margins. Paragraphs are left-aligned by
default. That is, their text lines up evenly at the left margin
but not the right margin. Right-aligned paragraphs, in

contrast, have a ragged left edge but form a straight line at the right margin. In centered paragraphs, each line is an equal distance from both the left and the right margins. Justified paragraphs line up in a straight line at both margins; extra space is added between words as required to make the text line up.

Note that Word considers a paragraph to be any amount of text—from a single letter to many sentences—followed by a paragraph mark, which you insert by pressing the ENTER key. (Paragraph marks are not displayed by default; for details, consult "View" under OPTIONS.) If you want to align a small amount of text such as a heading, just press ENTER after typing the text to be aligned, and then proceed with the alignment as just described. If you want to change the alignment of an entire document, first choose Edit, Select All (CTRL+A) and then issue the desired alignment command.

You can also align text around tabs; see TABS for further details.

Vertical Alignment

1. Choose File, Page Setup.
2. If necessary, choose the Layout tab.
3. Under Vertical Alignment, choose Top, Center, or Justified.
4. Under Apply To, choose which portion of the document you want to affect.
5. Click on OK or press ENTER.

Aligns the material in the current section vertically on the page, between the top and bottom margins. (In contrast, aligning text with the Format, Paragraph command determines how it is positioned between the left and right margins.) When you choose the Top setting for vertical alignment, Word aligns the selected material at the top margin; when you choose Center, Word aligns the selected material at an equal distance from the top and bottom margins; and if you choose Justified, Word aligns material so that the first paragraph begins at the top margin and the last paragraph ends at the bottom margin. You can also align selected text vertically, rather than the entire section. If you do, Word inserts section breaks as needed to set the selected text off from the rest of your document.

ALPHABETIZING

See SORTING TEXT.

ANNOTATIONS

You can add initialed and numbered annotations to a document. This is an excellent means of passing on comments to someone else or of writing notes to yourself that you don't want included in the body of the document.

You create annotations in a separate annotation pane that appears at the bottom of your screen. When this pane is closed, only an annotation mark (your initials plus a number, in hidden text form) appears within the text to indicate that an annotation is present. To view annotations for the active document, simply open the annotation pane to view the annotations associated with the visible area of the document. You can also view selected annotations, edit annotations, print them, add them to the body of the document, or discard them.

If you want others to be able to annotate your work but not change it, you can protect the document. (See PROTECTING DOCUMENTS.) You can also merge annotations into the original document so that the comments can be reviewed. (See REVISIONS.)

Creating Annotations

1. Place the insertion point in the desired spot or select some text you want to comment upon.
2. Choose Insert, Annotation.
3. Type annotation text in the annotation pane.
4. Click on Close or choose View, Annotations to close the annotation pane and return to your document.

Keyboard Shortcut:

ALT+CTRL+A   Opens the annotation pane and adds a blank entry to annotation list

Adds an annotation to the active document, inserts an annotation mark in the designated location in the text, and then closes the annotation pane. When you're through entering an annotation, you can also return to your document without closing the annotation pane by pressing F6 or clicking within the document.

The initials in the annotation mark are derived from the name you typed during installation. (See "User Info" under OPTIONS.) Within the text, annotation marks are displayed in hidden text form. If they are not visible on the screen, click on the Show/Hide button on the Standard toolbar. (Also see HIDDEN TEXT.)

Deleting Annotations

1. Within the document, select the annotation mark of the annotation to be deleted.
2. Press DEL or BACKSPACE.

Deletes the annotation mark in the text as well as the annotation itself. Any annotations after the deleted annotation are renumbered accordingly. For example, if you delete annotation DC1, annotation DC2 will become DC1. You must perform this operation within the document itself rather than within the annotation pane.

Editing Annotations

1. Choose View, Annotations if the annotation pane is not already displayed.
2. Edit and/or format the annotation text using standard editing and formatting procedures.
3. Click on Close to return to your document.

Enables you to modify existing annotations. You can edit the annotation text, but you cannot delete an annotation within the annotation pane. To delete annotations, see the preceding section.

Moving Annotations into the Text

1. Choose View, Annotations if the annotation pane is not displayed.
2. Select the annotation text to be moved (*do not* select the annotation mark itself).
3. Choose Edit, Copy or Edit, Cut.
4. Move the insertion point to the desired location in your document.
5. Choose Edit, Paste.

Copies selected text from the annotation pane into your document at the specified location. Use this technique if you decide to incorporate some annotation text into your document. Note that you can also copy or cut text from your document and place it in an annotation. See COPYING TEXT AND GRAPHICS and CUT AND PASTE for details.

Printing Annotations

To print annotations alone:

1. Choose File, Print.
2. Select Annotations under Print What.
3. Click on OK or press ENTER.

To print annotations along with document text:

1. Choose File, Print.
2. Make sure Document is selected under Print What.
3. Select Options.
4. Select Annotations under Include with Document.
5. Click on OK or press ENTER in the Options dialog box.
6. Click on OK or press ENTER in the Print dialog box.

Keyboard Shortcut:
CTRL+P   Opens the Print dialog box

Prints the annotations themselves, along with identifying page numbers; or else prints your document and then prints the annotations on a separate page. Once you have printed a document containing annotations, the relevant page numbers will show up in the annotation pane, and may need to be updated if your document changes substantially. See FIELDS and "Print" under OPTIONS for details.

Viewing Annotations

1. Choose View, Annotations.
2. To view annotations from a specific reviewer only, choose his or her name under From.

Mouse Shortcuts:
Double-click on   Opens annotation pane and moves to
annotation mark   selected annotation in annotation pane
in text

Double-click on annotation mark in annotation pane	Closes annotation pane and moves to selected annotation within body of document
	The Show/Hide button; displays annotation marks as well as other nonprinting characters, if they're not already displayed

Displays the annotation pane if it is not already displayed, and removes it from view if it is displayed. If you selected text in the document when creating an annotation, that text is selected again if you place the insertion point within the relevant annotation in the annotation pane.

If you don't see annotation marks within the text, click on the Show/Hide button on the Standard toolbar to bring them into view. If you see extra codes in the annotation pane (where normally just your initials, the annotation number, and perhaps a page number appear), you may have field codes on (see FIELDS).

You can also move the insertion point to a designated annotation with the Go To feature (see GO TO).

ARRANGE ALL

See WINDOWS.

ASCII

See SAVE AS.

AUTOCORRECT

1. Choose Tools, AutoCorrect.
2. Under Replace, enter the text that you want replaced automatically as you type. These AutoCorrect entry names can be up to 31 characters long, but cannot include spaces.
3. Under With, enter the replacement text.
4. Choose the Add button or press ENTER.

5. Enter any additional AutoCorrect entries in the same manner.

6. Click on OK or press ENTER.

Creates an AutoCorrect entry. Now when you type that word and then type a space, Word automatically inserts the replacement text into your document, provided that the AutoCorrect feature is enabled. (In contrast, you have to insert AutoText entries manually; see AUTOTEXT.) For example, if you frequently type the word "dunder" instead of "blunder," you could store that as an AutoCorrect entry. The next time you type dunder and then type a space, Word automatically changes it into "blunder." In addition, if you find a common typo during the course of a spell check, you can choose the AutoCorrect button to have Word add it—along with the correct spelling you suggest—to the list of AutoCorrect entries. (See SPELL CHECKING.)

You can also use the AutoCorrect feature to reduce your typing chores. For example, if you frequently have to type "United Bibliophiles of Greater Berkeley," you could create an AutoCorrect entry—UBGB, for example—that would tell Word to insert the entire name when you typed the abbreviation. Just make sure not to use AutoCorrect entry names (such as USE for "Union of Socialist Engineers") that are words you may use in some other context; Word will replace them in all cases when the AutoCorrect feature is activated.

When creating longer AutoCorrect entries, you can select the entry in your text before choosing Tools, AutoCorrect. The selected text will show up under With in the AutoCorrect dialog box. (Make sure Formatted Text is selected if the entry is longer than 255 characters; plain text entries are limited to 255 characters.)

In the AutoCorrect dialog box, you can also instruct Word to change which type of quotes are used, as well as having it ferret out words with two initial capital letters (usually these are typos), sentences without initial capital letters, and names of days that have not been capitalized.

You can also modify an AutoCorrect entry. To do so, first select the entry. (It's easiest to click on the word and its replacement at the bottom of the AutoCorrect dialog box.) Then type a new replacement word under With. At this point, the Add button changes to Replace, which you can choose to substitute the new AutoCorrect entry for the old.

You can disable the AutoCorrect feature by deselecting the Replace Text as You Type check box in the AutoCorrect dialog box. In addition, you can delete AutoCorrect entries that you no longer use by selecting them and choosing the Delete button.

AUTOFORMAT

1. To format only a portion of your document, select it; otherwise the entire document is formatted.
2. Choose Format, AutoFormat.
3. Click on OK or press ENTER.
4. Choose Accept, Reject All, Review Changes, or Style Gallery.

Keyboard Shortcut:

CTRL+K   Automatically formats document or selected text

Mouse Shortcut:

    Automatically formats document or selected text

Formats your document automatically using the preestablished styles for the template currently in effect (see STYLES and TEMPLATES). Word may also replace asterisks with bullet characters and straight quotes with curly ones. You can influence which types of changes AutoFormat will make; see "AutoFormat" under OPTIONS.

If you use the toolbar button or keyboard shortcut instead of the menu command, these changes are instituted without your input. (If necessary, you can reverse them with the Undo command.) If you use the menu command Format, AutoFormat, you can see the changes to your document after you click on OK in the AutoFormat dialog box. At this point you can accept, reject, or review the formatting changes.

Selecting Review Changes displays the Review AutoFormat Changes dialog box. From here, choose Hide Marks to conceal revision marks and see what the final document will look like, and Show Marks to reintroduce

the revision marks. (See REVISIONS.) Choose F<u>i</u>nd or
F<u>i</u>nd to review revisions one by one (either backward or
forward); any changes are mentioned under Description.
You can also use the vertical scroll bar to move through
your text and can then select the desired revisions. Select
R<u>e</u>ject to discard any revisions you dislike, and use <u>U</u>ndo
Last if you change your mind about revisions you have
rejected. Select the Find <u>N</u>ext after Reject check box to
have Word automatically move on to the next revision
after you reject a change. Once you're done, click on
Close or Cancel to return to the AutoFormat dialog box.

Selecting <u>S</u>tyle Gallery in the AutoFormat dialog box lets
you preview how your document would look with various
templates applied to it. (See STYLES and TEMPLATES.)
Note that there's also a separate command for formatting
tables automatically. (See TABLES.)

AUTOTEXT

Word's AutoText feature lets you create abbreviations for
passages of text that you use frequently. You can then
insert the entire text block into most documents just by
issuing the command to insert an AutoText entry. This can
cut down on your typing chores considerably. The
AutoCorrect feature offers an alternative way to insert text
automatically (see AUTOCORRECT).

Note that AutoText entries are shortcuts for repeated
text. To create shortcuts for a sequence of *commands*
that you repeat regularly, see MACROS. Also see
ORGANIZER for details on managing AutoText entries.

Creating AutoText Entries

1. Select the desired text.
2. Choose <u>E</u>dit, AutoTe<u>x</u>t.
3. Under <u>N</u>ame, type a name or edit the suggested name.
4. Click on <u>A</u>dd or press ENTER.

Mouse Shortcut:

  Displays the AutoText dialog box if text
is selected

Makes the selected text into an AutoText entry that you can later insert into the current document or any other document created with the same template. Make sure to use short names for your AutoText entries so it's easier to insert them, as described in a moment.

You cannot create an AutoText entry unless you first select some text. If you don't, the Add option in the AutoText dialog box will not be available. (If no AutoText entries have been created *and* no text has been selected, the AutoText option in the Edit menu will not be available.)

You can edit AutoText entries by inserting them into the text, making the desired changes, selecting the text, issuing the Edit, AutoText command, and using the name of the existing AutoText entry.

Deleting AutoText Entries

1. Choose Edit, AutoText.
2. Under Name, highlight the name of the AutoText entry to be deleted.
3. Click on the Delete button.

Deletes the selected AutoText entry so that you can no longer use it in any of your documents.

Inserting AutoText Entries

1. Position the insertion point where you want to place the AutoText entry.
2. Choose Edit, AutoText.
3. Under Name, highlight the name of the desired AutoText entry and click on Insert or press ENTER.

Keyboard Shortcut:

F3   Inserts the AutoText entry whose name you have just typed

Mouse Shortcut:

      Inserts the AutoText entry whose name you have just typed

Inserts the complete block of text associated with the AutoText entry you selected. For example, if you created an AutoText entry for your name and address, using any of the preceding methods would insert your complete

name and address into your document at the insertion point. The shortcut methods only work if you *first* type the AutoText name. (If the AutoText name for your name and address were DC, you could insert your name and address into the current document by typing DC and then either pressing F3 or clicking on the AutoText button.) Leave a space before the AutoText abbreviation, or Word will not be able to read it.

BACKUP

See SAVE.

BOLD

To boldface existing text:

1. Select the text to be boldfaced.
2. Choose Format, Font and click on the Font tab if necessary.
3. Choose Bold under Font Style.
4. Click on OK or press ENTER.

To boldface text as you type:

1. Place the insertion point where you want to type bold text.
2. Choose Format, Font and click on the Font tab if necessary.
3. Choose Bold under Font Style.
4. Click on OK or press ENTER.
5. Type the desired text.
6. Choose Format, Font.
7. Choose Regular under Font Style.
8. Click on OK or press ENTER.

Keyboard Shortcut:

CTRL+B   Boldfaces the selected text or the text you type (turns off boldfacing if it's already on)

Mouse Shortcut

B   Boldfaces the selected text or the text you type (turns off boldfacing if it's already on)

Creates characters that are darker than normal.
Boldfacing is an excellent device for headings and other
text that you want to stand out.

BOOKMARK

A *bookmark* is a place in your document that you name
and mark so you can easily return to it later. Bookmark
names can be up to 20 characters long, must start with a
letter, cannot include spaces, and must consist only of
letters, numbers, and the underscore. You can create a
bookmark at a particular insertion point. In addition, you
can select text to be used as a bookmark; when you
return to such bookmarks later, the text is once again
selected. Unlike annotations, bookmarks produce no
special character on screen.

Creating Bookmarks

1. Place the insertion point in the desired spot or select
   the text to be marked.
2. Choose Edit, Bookmark.
3. Type the bookmark name.
4. Click on Add or press ENTER.

Keyboard Shortcut:
CTRL+SHIFT+F5   Opens the Bookmark dialog box

Creates a bookmark in the designated location. Although
this produces no visible change on your screen, you can
easily return to that bookmark location later.

Deleting Bookmarks

1. Choose Edit, Bookmark.
2. Type or choose a bookmark name.
3. Choose the Delete button.
4. Click on the Close button or press ENTER.

Deletes the specified bookmark. This does not remove
any text from your document, but instead just removes
the bookmark itself so you cannot return to it later.

Finding Bookmarks

1. Choose Edit, Bookmark.
2. Under Bookmark Name, type or choose a bookmark name.
3. Click on Go To or press ENTER.
4. Click on Close or press ENTER to close the Bookmark dialog box.

Moves the insertion point to the bookmark you specify. If you selected text before creating the bookmark, that text is once again selected. You can also find bookmarks using the Go To feature (see GO TO).

Moving Bookmarks

1. Place the insertion point in the desired location or select the text to be marked.
2. Choose Edit, Bookmark.
3. Specify the name of the desired bookmark.
4. Choose the Add option.

Moves the bookmark from its previous location to the new location as indicated by the insertion point or text selection.

BORDERS

You can place borders around paragraphs, tables, cells in a table, and graphics that you insert into your document. Since a paragraph is any amount of text followed by a paragraph mark, you can place a border around a sentence, or even a word, if you follow it with a paragraph mark by pressing ENTER. You can also apply shading within the borders around text or tables, but not graphics. (See SHADING.)

Creating Four-Sided Borders

1. Select the paragraph(s), table, table cells, or graphic around which you want to place a border.
2. Choose Format, Borders and Shading, and select the Borders tab if necessary.
3. Under Presets, choose a border style.

4. Under Style, choose a line style for the border.

5. Click on OK or press ENTER.

Mouse Shortcuts:

 Displays Borders toolbar, or hides it if it is already displayed

 Inserts four-sided border of designated style and line type around selected object

Places a four-sided, rectangular border around the selected text, table cells, table, or graphic.

If the Borders toolbar is not already displayed, click on the Show Toolbar button in the Borders and Shading dialog box to display it. You can use this toolbar to introduce borders, and to select line styles, border styles, and shading.

Borders that you apply to a paragraph extend from the right to the left indent, no matter how much text there is per line. To produce a smaller box, increase the indents (see INDENTATION). You can also change the From Text setting to move the border closer to or farther from the text.

Under Preset, you can choose between the border types None, Box, or Shadow for text and graphics. If you've selected two or more cells in a table, the Shadow option is replaced with Grid, which enables you to place borders around individual table cells.

Choose from the selections in the Color drop-down list box if you want to change the color of lines used in the border and you have a color monitor or color printer (see COLORS).

The Border box displays the currently selected options. To clear unwanted settings, click on None under Presets; this resets both the border style and the line style to None.

Note that you can edit existing borders by selecting the text, table, or graphic that has a border, and then following the preceding steps.

Creating Lines with the Border Feature

1. Select the desired paragraph(s), table, table cells, or graphic.

2. Choose Format, Borders and Shading, and select the Borders tab if necessary.

3. Under Presets, choose <u>N</u>one.
4. Under St<u>y</u>le, select the desired line style.
5. Under Bo<u>r</u>der, click on the sides on which you want a line to appear.
6. Click on OK or press ENTER.

Mouse Shortcuts:

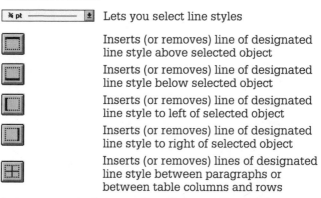

⅜ pt ━━━━━ ⬇	Lets you select line styles
⊡	Inserts (or removes) line of designated line style above selected object
⊡	Inserts (or removes) line of designated line style below selected object
⊡	Inserts (or removes) line of designated line style to left of selected object
⊡	Inserts (or removes) line of designated line style to right of selected object
⊞	Inserts (or removes) lines of designated line style between paragraphs or between table columns and rows

Lets you create lines—rather than a rectangular border—on selected sides of the paragraph, table, table cells, or graphic in question. For example, you can create lines at the top and bottom of a graphic. (First select a line style, and then select multiple buttons on the Borders toolbar to introduce borders on several sides of the selected object.) If you've selected multiple paragraphs, you can insert lines between paragraphs by clicking to introduce a line in the middle of the Bo<u>r</u>der box or by using the appropriate button on the Borders toolbar.

The selection triangles in the Bo<u>r</u>der box indicate which side(s) will be affected if you select a new line style. Normally, clicking on one side deselects any other selected sides. However, you can select a side without deselecting any others by holding down SHIFT while you click.

You can create borders with different line types on different sides. To do so, select <u>N</u>one under Presets in the Borders and Shading dialog box. Select a line style and, under Bo<u>r</u>der, click on the sides to which you want to apply that style. Then select a side that will have a different line style, choose a new line style, and click on other sides to apply the new line style. If you're using the Borders toolbar, select

line styles *before* selecting the buttons representing
particular borders.

Removing Borders

1. Select the text, table, or graphic whose border you want
   to remove.
2. Choose Format, Borders and Shading, and select the
   Borders tab if necessary.
3. Choose None under Preset to remove all borders,
   or click on lines under Border to remove just
   those borders.
4. Click on OK or press ENTER.

Mouse Shortcut:

 Deletes all borders around selected object

Removes all borders or the designated borders. Most of
the Borders toolbar buttons also enable you either to add
or remove particular borders.

BREAKS

See COLUMNS, PAGE BREAKS, and SECTIONS.

BULLETS

Bulleted lists are an excellent organizational device, and
can help draw attention to a number of items or to a
series of points. You can also add a unique touch to your
work by choosing an unusual bullet character. See
MULTILEVEL LISTS NUMBERED LISTS, and OUTLINING,
for other ways to organize your thoughts.

Adding Bullets

1. Select the paragraphs you want to precede
   with bullets.
2. Choose Format, Bullets and Numbering.
3. If necessary, select the Bulleted tab.
4. Choose one of the bullet styles.
5. Make sure Hanging Indent is selected if you want the
   paragraphs to have a hanging indent.
6. Click on OK or press ENTER.

Mouse Shortcut:

 Inserts bullets in front of selected paragraphs, or removes bullets if they're already there

Inserts the designated bullet character in front of the selected paragraphs. Paragraphs can consist of any amount of text followed by a paragraph mark, so you can use this method to place bullets in front of single words or short phrases if you like.

Selecting Modify in the Bullet and Numbering dialog box displays the Modify Bulleted List dialog box, in which you can change the bullet's point size, position, and color. You can also select Bullet in this dialog box to change the bullet character, as described next.

Defining New Bullet Characters

1. Choose Format, Bullets and Numbering.
2. If necessary, select the Bulleted tab.
3. Choose Modify, under Bullet Character choose the bullet to be replaced with a new bullet character, and then choose Bullet.
4. Choose a new bullet character.
5. Click on OK or press ENTER.

Replaces the selected bullet in the Modify Bulleted List dialog box with the character you pick from the Symbol dialog box. To insert the new bullet character into your document, select it and choose OK or press ENTER. (The bullet that is selected when you close this dialog box becomes the default bullet used when you select the Bullet button on the Formatting toolbar.) You can change as many of these available bullet characters as you like. The new bullet styles remain available in the Modify Bulleted List dialog box until you change them again.

In the Symbol dialog box, choose from the Symbols From drop-down list box to see alternate sets of available bullet characters. Select a character set and then choose from those characters as described above. Also see SYMBOLS for more information.

Removing Bullets

1. Select the bulleted paragraphs.
2. Choose Format, Bullets and Numbering.

3. If necessary, select the <u>B</u>ulleted tab.

4. Choose the <u>R</u>emove button.

Mouse Shortcut:

 Removes the bullet characters—as well as the hanging indent, if applicable—from the selected paragraphs.

CANCEL

See "Canceling Commands" under "General Procedures"; *also see* UNDO.

CAPITALIZATION

1. Select the text to be changed.

2. Choose F<u>o</u>rmat, Change Cas<u>e</u>.

3. Choose <u>S</u>entence case., <u>l</u>owercase, <u>U</u>PPERCASE, <u>T</u>itle Case, or t<u>O</u>GGLE cASE.

4. Click on OK or press ENTER.

Keyboard Shortcut:

SHIFT+F3   Cycles selected text between uppercase, lowercase, and sentence case

Changes the capitalization of the selected text. <u>S</u>entence case. produces an uppercase letter at the beginning of each sentence (any amount of text followed by a period, a question mark, or an exclamation point). <u>l</u>owercase produces all lowercase text, and <u>U</u>PPERCASE produces all uppercase text. <u>T</u>itle Case produces uppercase letters at the beginning of each word, and t<u>O</u>GGLE cASE changes uppercase letters to lowercase and lowercase letters to uppercase.

You can also use the Font dialog box to change the case of existing lowercase text or of text that you type

1. Choose the text to be modified if applicable.

2. Choose F<u>o</u>rmat, <u>F</u>ont.

3. Choose the Fo<u>n</u>t tab if necessary.

4. Choose S<u>m</u>all Caps or <u>A</u>ll Caps under Effects.

5. Click on OK or press ENTER.

Keyboard Shortcuts:

CTRL+SHIFT+A	Toggles selected lowercase text between uppercase and lowercase
CTRL+SHIFT+K	Toggles selected lowercase text between small capitals and lowercase

Changes the case of the selected text or the text you type to uppercase or small capitals. If you're typing new text in small capitals or uppercase, make sure to turn the feature off once you're done by repeating these steps but deselecting the Small Caps or All Caps check box.

Creating Drop Capitals

1. Switch to Page Layout view.
2. Select the letter (or letters) that you want to make into a drop cap.
3. Choose Format, Drop Cap.
4. Under Position, choose Dropped or In Margin.
5. If applicable, choose a new font under Font.
6. Under Lines to Drop, choose how far down to extend the letter.
7. Under Distance from Text, choose how far from the drop capital the text to its right will begin.
8. Click on OK or press ENTER.

Creates a drop capital letter. You can only create such letters at the beginning of a paragraph, and you can only see a drop cap as it will be printed if you're in Page Layout view or in Print Preview. Used sparingly, drop caps can add style to your work; they are particularly well suited to chapter openings or section beginnings.

To remove a dropped capital letter, simply select the dropped capital you want to remove and follow the preceding steps, but choose None under Position.

CAPTIONS

1. Select the object for which to insert a caption.
2. Choose Insert, Caption.
3. Under Caption, type caption text after the caption number.

4. Under Label, pick the appropriate label type.
5. Under Position, determine where to place the caption.
6. Click on OK or press ENTER.

Inserts a numbered and labeled caption associated with the selected item. Word numbers these captions automatically, and numbers different types of items independently (tables are numbered separately from figures). If you want to edit a caption's text after the fact, just edit it on your document screen; don't try to use the Caption dialog box or you'll insert an extra caption. Also, don't try to edit the caption number on the screen. It's a field that Word renumbers automatically as necessary (see FIELDS).

Choose New Label in the Caption dialog box if you need a new label type, such as Box. Choose Numbering to change the numbering scheme, and choose AutoCaption to have Word add captions automatically when you insert objects.

CENTER

See ALIGNMENT.

CHARACTER FORMATTING

See BOLD, CAPITALIZATION, FONT, HIDDEN TEXT, ITALIC, SPACING, STRIKETHROUGH, SUBSCRIPT AND SUPERSCRIPT, and UNDERLINING.

CHARTS

See GRAPHS.

CLEAR

See DELETING TEXT AND GRAPHICS.

CLIPBOARD

The *Clipboard*—a Windows feature available in all
Windows programs—is a temporary holding place for
text, tables, or graphics. You can insert material from the
Clipboard into any area in your document, and even into
other documents or other Windows applications. The
Clipboard is the ideal means of transferring information.

You place material in the Clipboard with the Edit, Cut or
Edit, Copy command. (Cut removes the original from the
document and places it in the Clipboard; Copy places a
copy in the Clipboard but leaves the original intact.) You
insert material from the Clipboard into a document via
the Edit, Paste (or Edit, Paste Special) command.
Whatever you place in the Clipboard resides there until
you replace it by cutting or copying something else. This
enables you to paste material from the Clipboard
repeatedly—sometimes cutting down on your typing
chores considerably.

If you want to move several blocks of text and/or
graphics at a time, you can use the Spike (see SPIKE).
Also see COPYING TEXT AND GRAPHICS, CUT AND
PASTE, EMBEDDING, and LINKING.

CLOSING FILES

1. Choose File, Close.
2. If necessary, respond to any prompts that appear.

Keyboard Shortcut:
CTRL+F4   Closes the active document window

Mouse Shortcut:

| Double-click on the document window's Control menu box | Closes the active document window |

Closes the active document window—removing it from
the screen (and from memory) without leaving Word for
Windows. If there are unsaved changes to the active
document, Word asks if you want to save them. Answer
Yes to save the changes and close the document, No to
discard the changes and close the document, Cancel to

cancel the operation and return to the active document, and Help for help on the current operation. To close all open files, hold down SHIFT while opening the File menu and choose Close All.

If the document you're closing is the only open document, you'll see a blank screen with an abbreviated menu bar. If the document you're closing is one of many open documents, closing it returns you to another open document. See also "Opening and Closing Files" under "General Procedures."

COLORS

You can change the color of text and borders in Word for Windows. This feature is only relevant if you have a color monitor, a color printer, or both.

Border Color

1. Select the text, table, or graphic whose border color you wish to change.
2. Choose Format, Borders and Shading, and click on the Borders tab, if necessary.
3. Pull down the Color drop-down list box and select the desired color.
4. Click on OK or press ENTER.

Changes the color of the border around the selected item. You can also choose a border color as you create a border. See BORDERS for details.

Text Color

1. Select the text to be changed.
2. Choose Format, Font.
3. If necessary, click on the Font tab.
4. Choose a color from the Color drop-down list box.
5. Click on OK or press ENTER.

Changes the color of text that you type, provided that you have the appropriate color monitor and video display adapter. You can also change the color of text as you type. Just use the preceding method to turn on the color (make sure no text is selected) and then type the desired text. When you're done, follow the previous steps but choose Auto to restore the default text color.

COLUMNS

You can create two types of columns in Word: newspaper columns, where text fills one column before flowing to the top of the next, and table columns, which consist of individual cells into which you can enter lists of information (see TABLES). You can divide existing text into columns, or you can create a new column layout and then begin to type. When working with newspaper-type columns, switch to Page Layout view or Print Preview so you can see the columns side by side.

Creating Columns

1. If necessary, choose View, Page Layout to switch to Page Layout view.

2. Place the insertion point in the appropriate location or select the desired text.

3. Choose Format, Columns.

4. Choose a column layout under Presets, or select the desired number of columns in the Number of Columns box.

5. If you want to alter column widths and the spacing between columns, change the values under Width and Spacing. To create columns of unequal widths, first deselect the Equal Column Width check box.

6. Select the Line Between check box if you want to create a vertical line between columns.

7. Select the Start New Column check box if you want to start a new column at the insertion point.

8. Under Apply To, choose which portion of the document you want to format with columns.

9. Click on OK or press ENTER.

Mouse Shortcut:

 Click on this button, drag across the displayed grid to choose the number of columns, then release the mouse button

Divides the specified portion of text into the designated number of columns. To remove columns, just choose

Format, Columns, One, or select a one-column layout using the Columns button on the Standard toolbar.

You can also use the mouse to adjust the widths of existing columns by dragging on the right or left edge of the rectangular column width markers that appear on the ruler when you create columns. Increase the size of a column width marker to increase the space between columns, and decrease its size to reduce the amount of space between columns.

Creating Columns of Even Lengths

1. Place the insertion point right after the shorter column.
2. Choose Insert, Break.
3. Choose Continuous under Section Breaks.
4. Click on OK or press ENTER.

Redistributes text to create columns of even lengths. Use this technique when the rightmost column on the last page of your document is not completely filled with text. Place the insertion point at the end of the final (shorter) column, but before any subsequent section breaks. (See SECTIONS.)

Inserting Column Breaks

1. Place the insertion point where you want to break the column.
2. Choose Insert, Break.
3. Choose Column Break.
4. Click on OK or press ENTER.

Keyboard Shortcut: CTRL+SHIFT+ENTER

Moves text after the column break to the next column, whether or not the current column has been filled with text. (This is analogous to inserting a hard page break before you entirely fill a page with text; see PAGE BREAKS.) You only need to issue this command if you want to move on to the next column at a specific point in the text. Otherwise, Word for Windows "wraps" text to the next column when it reaches the end of a column—much as it wraps regular text to the next line when it reaches the right edge of a page.

Using Various Numbers of Columns in a Document

To create documents that contain differing numbers of columns in different areas, first divide the document into separate sections. (See SECTIONS.) Then use the methods just described to apply the desired number of columns in the individual sections. You can even have separate sections—and thus different numbers of columns—on a single page.

COPYING FILES

1. Choose File, Find File.
2. If necessary, search for the desired files (see FINDING FILES).
3. Under Listed Files in the Find File dialog box, highlight the file or files to be copied.
4. Choose Commands and select Copy.
5. In the Copy dialog box, type or select the drive and directory in which to store the file(s).
6. Click on OK or press ENTER.
7. Choose Close to exit from the Find File dialog box.

Enables you to place a copy of one or more files on a different drive and/or directory. (Select New in the Copy dialog box to create a new directory into which to copy the files.) This feature is handy for copying files to a floppy-disk drive for backup purposes. You can copy multiple files by selecting the desired files before proceeding with the copy operation. For more details, see FINDING FILES.

COPYING TEXT AND GRAPHICS

1. Select the text, table, or graphic to be copied.
2. Choose Edit, Copy.
3. Place the insertion point where you want to insert the copied material.
4. Choose Edit, Paste.

Keyboard Shortcuts:

CTRL+C or   Copies selected material to the Clipboard
CTRL+INS

CTRL+V or   Pastes material from the Clipboard into the
SHIFT+INS   document at insertion point

Mouse Shortcuts:

    Copies selected material to the Clipboard

    Pastes material from the Clipboard into the
                        document at insertion point

Copies the selected text, table, or graphic to the Clipboard—a temporary storage area—without removing the original from the document. (See CLIPBOARD.) Once you've copied material to the Clipboard, you can insert (paste) it anywhere in the document, or even into another document or another Windows application.

You don't need to open both documents at once to copy data between them. However, if you're transferring lots of material from one document to another, you may want to display them both at once. (See WINDOWS.)

The "Smart Cut and Paste" feature adds and removes spaces when necessary when you cut (or copy) and paste. You can turn this option off if you prefer; see "Edit" under OPTIONS.

Here is an alternative means of copying text with the mouse that does not make use of the Clipboard. You can use this technique to copy text within a document, or between two or more documents displayed on the screen. You cannot, however, use it to copy tables or to copy information between applications.

1. Select the text or graphic to be copied.
2. Point to the place you want to insert a copy (but *do not* click yet).
3. Press CTRL+SHIFT and click the *right* mouse button.

Also see DRAG AND DROP for instructions on an alternate means of copying text, tables, or graphics using the mouse.

CROSS-REFERENCES

1. Place the insertion point where you want to insert the cross-reference.

2. Choose Insert, Cross-reference.

3. Under Reference Type, choose what type of item you're going to be referring to.

4. Under Insert Reference To, choose which aspect of the item you'll be referring to—such as page number, caption, or footnote number.

5. Under For Which, choose the specific item you want to refer to.

6. Click on Insert or press ENTER.

7. When you're done inserting cross-references, click on Close or Cancel.

Inserts a cross-reference of the designated type in the selected location. For example, within the text of your document you could refer to a particular footnote, and list what page it falls on. If any of this information—such as page number and caption name—changes in the future, you can make sure the changes are reflected in your cross-reference by selecting the entire document and pressing F9 to update all fields (see FIELDS).

CUSTOMIZE

You can customize the Word for Windows toolbars, menus, and available keyboard shortcuts to suit your taste and the needs of your work.

Customizing Keyboard Shortcuts

1. Choose Tools, Customize.

2. If necessary, click on the Keyboard tab.

3. Under Categories, select a command category.

4. Under Commands, select the command for which you want to create a new shortcut key.

5. Place the insertion point under Press New Shortcut Key and press a new key combination.

6. Click on Assign or press ENTER.

7. When you're done assigning new shortcut keys, click on Close or press ENTER.

Assigns a shortcut keystroke combination to the selected command. If you select Press New Shortcut Key and press a shortcut key that's already in use, Word informs you which command it's currently assigned to. You can reassign it to the selected command, but then it will no longer work for the original command to which it was assigned.

To get rid of a shortcut, select the command it's assigned to (under Commands), select the shortcut under Current Keys, and then choose Remove.

Customizing Menus

1. Choose Tools, Customize.
2. If necessary, click on the Menus tab.
3. Under Categories, select a command category.
4. Under Change What Menu, select the menu to which you want to add a command or the menu that contains the command whose name you want to change.
5. Under Commands, select the command that you want to add or rename.
6. Click on Add if you want to add the command.
7. Use Name on Menu to change the name that appears on the menu for the currently selected command.
8. Use Position on Menu to choose a menu location for the selected menu command.
9. When you're done customizing the menu layout, click on Close or press ENTER.

Enables you to add selections to menus, and to customize the name and location of selected menu commands. You can use this technique to modify the menu system to suit your work style. (Note that the Name on Menu option is not available for certain of the original menu commands.) You can use the Menu Bar button to change the order of menus in the menu bar at the top of the screen. If you customize the menu system and later have a change of heart, you can use the Remove option to remove the currently selected command from the menus. To restore the original menu commands as established by Microsoft, choose the Reset All button.

Customizing the Toolbars

1. Make sure any toolbar you want to modify is displayed on the screen.

2. Choose Tools, Customize.

3. If necessary, click on the Toolbars tab.

4. Make a selection under Categories to display the available buttons.

5. Under Buttons, click on buttons if you want to see their descriptions in the lower-left corner of the dialog box.

6. Drag buttons from the Customize dialog box onto the toolbar in question, releasing the mouse button where you want to insert the new toolbar button.

Permits you to customize any toolbars that are currently displayed on the screen. Note that adding buttons may push other buttons off the toolbar. While the Customize dialog box is displayed, you can get rid of buttons to make room for new ones by dragging them off of the toolbar, and you can rearrange buttons by dragging them to a new spot on the toolbar. You can also move toolbar buttons when the Customize dialog box is not displayed by dragging them while holding down ALT. If you want to add buttons to a new (rather than an existing) toolbar, choose View, Toolbars, New. Then name the toolbar and add buttons to it as just described. (See TOOLBARS.)

You can add items other than existing buttons to toolbars. For example, if you select AutoText under Categories, you can add AutoText entries to the toolbar of your choice simply by dragging them onto the toolbar, as described above. Word will display the Custom Button dialog box, and you can assign a button to the item by highlighting the desired button and clicking on Assign or pressing ENTER.

CUT AND PASTE

1. Select the text, table, or graphic to be cut.

2. Choose Edit, Cut.

3. Place the insertion point where you want to insert the text, table, or graphic you cut.

4. Choose Edit, Paste.

Keyboard Shortcuts:

CTRL+X or   Cuts selected material to the Clipboard
SHIFT+DEL

CTRL+V or   Pastes material from Clipboard into document
SHIFT+INS   at insertion point

Mouse Shortcuts:

 Cuts selected material to the Clipboard

 Pastes material from the Clipboard into the document at insertion point

Cuts the selected text, table, or graphic to the Clipboard—a temporary storage area—and removes the original from the document. Once you've cut material to the Clipboard, you can insert (paste) it into any location in the document, or even into another document or another Windows application.

You don't need to open both documents at once to move data between them with the Cut command. You can instead cut the desired text, then open the document you want to paste the text into, and finally execute the paste operation. However, if you're moving lots of material from one document to another, you may want to open them both and make both visible. (See WINDOWS.)

The "Smart Cut and Paste" feature adds and removes spaces when necessary when you cut (or copy) and paste. You can turn this option off if you prefer; see "Edit" under OPTIONS.

Also see DRAG AND DROP for instructions on an alternate means of cutting and pasting text using the mouse. And see SPIKE for information on a way of cutting and pasting several items at a time.

DATE AND TIME

1. Place the insertion point in desired location.
2. Choose Insert, Date and Time.
3. Under Available Formats, choose a date or time format and click on OK or press ENTER.

Keyboard Shortcuts:

ALT+SHIFT+D   Inserts the current date
ALT+SHIFT+T   Inserts the current time

Inserts the date or time (according to your computer's clock) into your document in the requested format. If you select the Insert as Field check box, the date or time will be inserted as a field. You can update this field to insert the current time or date, or you can replace it with its current results so that it cannot be changed later (see FIELDS). If you see codes rather than a date or time in your document, you have field codes displayed. See "View" under OPTIONS for details. You can also add dates to headers and footers. (See HEADERS AND FOOTERS.)

DELETING FILES

1. Choose File, Find File.
2. If necessary, search for the desired files (see FINDING FILES).
3. Under Listed Files, highlight the desired files.
4. Choose Commands and select Delete.
5. Respond Yes or press ENTER at the prompt.

Deletes the selected file or files. Note that you cannot delete open files. You can delete multiple files by selecting the files in question before initiating the delete operation. For more details on finding files and selecting files in the Find File dialog box, see FINDING FILES.

You can use Delete in conjunction with the Copy option in the Find File dialog box to move files from one location to another: Simply copy the files to a new location and then delete them from their original location.

There are ways of protecting files from changes or deletion. See OPENING FILES, PASSWORDS, and PROTECTING DOCUMENTS.

DELETING TEXT AND GRAPHICS

1. Select the text, table, or graphic to be deleted.
2. Choose Edit, Clear.

Keyboard Shortcut:
DEL or BACKSPACE   Deletes the selected text

Deletes the selected text, table, or graphic. Additional methods of deleting text are covered in "Deleting Text" under "General Procedures." See also CUT AND PASTE and SPIKE for discussions of how to delete text, tables, or graphics from one location and reintroduce them in another.

If you accidentally delete an item, you can reverse the operation by choosing the Undo command from the Edit menu or using the Undo button on the Standard toolbar.

You can also protect your text from deletion. See OPENING FILES, PASSWORDS, and PROTECTING DOCUMENTS.

DICTIONARY

See LANGUAGE, SPELL CHECKING.

DIRECTORIES

1. Choose Tools, Options.
2. Choose the File Locations tab.
3. Select the file type whose location (default directory) you want to change.
4. Click on Modify.
5. Choose a new location for the selected file type.
6. Click on OK and then choose Close in the Options dialog box.

Changes the default directory that is used for the selected group of files. For example, if you select the subdirectory WINWORD\LETTERS for all document files, the Open dialog box will display files in the LETTERS subdirectory, and document files that you save will automatically be placed in the LETTERS subdirectory.

If you don't see the desired directory in the Modify Location dialog box, you can double-click on a parent directory to display all of its subdirectories. In addition, you can create a new directory by clicking on the New button and entering a directory name.

DRAG AND DROP

1. Select the text, table, or graphic to be moved.
2. Drag the item to a new location in the document.
3. Release the mouse button to insert the text, table, or graphic in the designated spot.

Moves the selected item. (You can also copy the selected item by holding down the CTRL key while dragging.) As you drag, you'll see a box-like icon attached to the lower-right portion of the mouse pointer (and a plus sign to the pointer's right if you hold down the CTRL key), plus a dotted insertion point (vertical bar) showing where the selected item will be placed if you release the mouse button at that point. You can turn drag-and-drop off or on. Choose Options from the Tools menu, click on the Edit tab, and either select or deselect the Drag-and-Drop Text Editing check box.

You can use the drag-and-drop feature to move or copy text between documents—if both are visible on the screen—as well as within a single document. You can drag text to a location off screen; the screen scrolls as you drag. However, it can be impractical to drag text over long distances within a document. For other means of moving or copying text, see COPYING TEXT AND GRAPHICS, CUT AND PASTE, and SPIKE.

EMBEDDING

The Object command on Word's Insert menu enables you to insert information—including text, data, charts, and graphics—from other sources into Word. You can either retrieve existing data from another application, or activate another application from within Word, create an object, and then insert it into Word.

Objects inserted in this manner are *embedded* in Word. This means that they are actually a part of the Word file (unlike linked files), but also retain an association with the source application in which they were created. When you double-click on an embedded object, Word opens the original application (assuming it's installed), lets you edit in that environment, and then permits you to return to Word, where your changes will be put into place. (Note that this does not change the original copy from another source.) Use embedding when you want to actually include an object from another source within a Word document. Use linking rather than embedding to share data between applications—that is, to ensure that a single set of data exists, and remains up to date, both in Word and in its source application. (See LINKING.)

Embedding Objects

To embed existing objects into Word:

1. Place the insertion point in the desired location.
2. Choose Insert, Object.
3. Click on the Create from File tab, if necessary.
4. Choose the desired file under File Name. If necessary, switch drives and/or directories—or click on Find File—to hunt down the file you're looking for.
5. Click on OK or press ENTER.

To embed new objects into Word:

1. Choose Insert, Object.
2. Click on the Create New tab, if necessary.
3. Under Object Type, choose the desired application.
4. Click on OK or press ENTER.
5. Create an object in the application you've just opened.
6. When you're done, choose File, Exit or click within the Word document to return to Word. If necessary, save and/or update the object when prompted.

Embeds an object within Word. You can choose the Display as Icon option if you want to see the embedded object as an icon within Word. (The Change Icon button that appears lets you change which icon is displayed.)

You can also use the Edit, Paste Special command to embed some or all of an existing file:

1. Get into the application from which you want to gather material and open the desired file.
2. Select the material to be embedded; you can select any portion of the file.
3. Choose Edit, Copy.
4. Switch into Word. (If you're not sure how to switch between applications, see your Windows documentation.)
5. Place the insertion point where you want to insert the embedded material.
6. Choose Edit, Paste Special.

7. Make sure the Paste option button is selected, and, under As, choose the option that includes the word "object."

8. Click on OK or press ENTER.

Embeds the selected material within your document. In the Paste Special dialog box, make certain to pick a selection that includes the word "object," or the object will not actually be embedded—that is, you won't be able to edit it within its native application just by double-clicking on it in Word.

Modifying Embedded Objects in the Source Application

1. Open your Word document and select the embedded object to be edited.

2. Choose Edit, Object, and then choose Edit from the submenu that appears. (The Object command may have a more specific name, such as Microsoft Excel Worksheet Object.)

3. Edit the object as desired, using all the tools available in its application of origin.

4. When you're done, choose File, Exit or click within the Word document to return to Word. If necessary, update and/or save the object when prompted.

Mouse Shortcut:

Double-click on the embedded object	Opens the source application

Enables you to edit the embedded object in the application in which it was created, and have those changes reflected in the Word document. You can also modify embedded objects to some extent within Word (see GRAPHICS).

ENDNOTES

See FOOTNOTES.

ENVELOPES

1. Open the document that contains the letter for which you're creating an envelope.
2. Choose Tools, Envelopes and Labels.
3. Choose the Envelopes tab if necessary.
4. If necessary, enter the recipient's address under Delivery Address.
5. If you need to, enter a return address under Return Address.
6. Click on Print to print the envelope.

Creates and prints an envelope either for the current letter or for a letter that you plan to type. If you need to select an envelope size or change any printing options, choose Options in the Envelopes and Labels dialog box and make the desired selections in the Envelope Options dialog box, choosing OK when you're done.

If you select text before issuing the Tools, Envelopes and Labels command, Word automatically inserts that text in the Delivery Address box. Word also inserts your return address automatically using the address listed under User Info in the Options dialog box (see OPTIONS). Select the Omit check box in the Envelopes and Labels dialog box to prevent this return address from printing.

You can add the envelope to your document by choosing the Add to Document button. This adds a section to the beginning of your document with the address and, if applicable, the return address (Word automatically selects the envelope size). The Add to Document button becomes Change Document if you've already inserted an envelope section into your document. This permits you to change the information for that envelope. First make your changes in the Envelope and Labels dialog box, and then choose Change Document to put the changes into place.

For information on printing mailing labels, see LABELS and MAIL MERGE.

EXIT

See "Leaving Word for Windows" under "General Procedures."

FIELDS

A *field* is a code or set of codes that instructs Word to insert specified information into your document. For instance, you can insert a field that tells Word to place the date in your document at that location. The great advantage of fields is that you can update them automatically. You can use fields to insert dates, page numbers, graphics, text blocks, and even entire files into your document. Word also uses fields to build indexes, tables of contents, and more.

Some commands—including many of the commands on the Insert menu—insert field codes automatically. In addition, you can insert codes manually using the Insert, Field command; this method allows a far wider range of actions but requires more knowledge on your part. An in-depth coverage of fields is beyond the scope of this book. For details, consult your documentation or on-line help.

Adding Fields

1. Place the insertion point in the desired location.
2. Choose Insert, Field.
3. Under Categories, choose a field type or choose [All] to display all fields.
4. Under Field Names, select the desired field.
5. Click on OK or press ENTER.

Keyboard Shortcut:

CTRL+F9   Inserts empty field character ({}), into which you can type a field name and field instructions (press F9 when you're done)

Inserts the designated field at the insertion point. If you see codes rather than the expected results, see "Viewing Field Codes and Field Results" later in this section. If you want to insert additional instructions, either type them in the Field Codes box or click on Options and make selections from the Field Options dialog box that appears. When you're done, choose OK to return to the Field dialog box.

Deleting Fields

1. Select the field or fields to be deleted.
2. Press DEL or BACKSPACE.

Deletes the selected field or fields. You can delete fields even if they are locked (see "Locking Fields").

Fields are shaded by default when the insertion point is anywhere within them, but this does not mean that they are selected. When you select a field, it is also shaded but its text is displayed in white rather than black. Before attempting to delete a field, make sure that it is selected rather than just shaded. You can turn off this automatic field shading if you find it confusing (see "View" under OPTIONS).

Editing Fields

1. Place the insertion point in the field to be edited.
2. Make sure that field codes are displayed (press SHIFT+F9 if necessary).
3. Edit the codes as needed.
4. Press SHIFT+F9 to see field results.
5. Press F9 to update the field.

Modifies the selected field. You might do this, for example, to alter a field that makes a calculation. You may want to delve into fields a bit more before you experiment with editing. Consult the Word for Windows documentation or on-line help system for details about the available field codes, along with their uses, syntax, instructions, and any arguments.

Finding Fields

To go to the next field:

1. Press F11.

To go to the previous field:

1. Press SHIFT+F11.

Moves the insertion point to the next or previous field. This technique works regardless of whether the fields are displayed as field codes or field results. Note, however, that Word passes over fields—such as index entries and table of contents entries—that are formatted as hidden text.

You can also hunt for field codes using the Go To or Find feature (see GO TO and FINDING TEXT, FORMATTING, AND SPECIAL CHARACTERS). In addition, you can display fields as codes rather than results, or turn on shading for field codes, to make it easier to find fields as you browse through your document. See "Viewing Field Codes and Field Results."

Locking Fields

To lock one or more fields:

1. Position the insertion point within the field or select the fields to be locked.
2. Press CTRL+F11.

To unlock one or more fields:

1. Position the insertion point within the field or select the fields to be unlocked.
2. Press CTRL+SHIFT+F11.

Locking fields temporarily prevents you from updating them; unlocking fields enables you to update them once again. You can lock and unlock fields whether they are displayed as field codes or field results. Locking a field produces no visible change on the screen; if you try to update a locked field with F9, however, the field is not changed.

Unlinking Fields

1. Position the insertion point within a field or select the desired fields.
2. Press CTRL+SHIFT+F9.

"Unlinks" the designated fields—that is, changes them into their results (in the form of regular text) so that you cannot update them automatically in the future. You can unlink fields whether they are displayed as field codes or field results. Unlike locking a field, unlinking a field permanently prevents it from being updated. You can, however, reverse the unlink operation with an undo command (see UNDO).

Updating Fields

1. Place the mouse pointer over the field, or select the entire document to update all fields.
2. Right-click on the field to display a shortcut menu.
3. Choose Update Field.

Keyboard Shortcut:

F9   Updates the field containing the insertion point, or all selected fields

Updates the designated field or fields to obtain their current results. For example, you could update a time or date field to obtain the current time or date. You can also lock or unlink fields so that they cannot be updated, as described earlier.

To stipulate that fields be updated automatically when you print

1. Choose Tools, Options.
2. If necessary, click on the Print tab.
3. Select the Update Fields check box and click on OK or press ENTER.

Viewing Field Codes and Field Results

To view field codes or field results for the entire document:

1. Choose Tools, Options.
2. If necessary, select the View tab.
3. Select the Field Codes check box to view field codes, or deselect it to view field results.
4. Click on OK or press ENTER.

Keyboard Shortcut:

ALT+F9   Switches entire document between display of field codes and field results

To view field codes or field results for one or more selected fields:

1. Place the insertion point within the field or select the fields.
2. Right-click on a field to display a shortcut menu.
3. Select Toggle Field Codes to turn on or off the display of field codes for the designated field(s).

Keyboard Shortcut:

SHIFT+F9 Alternately displays field codes and field results for the designated fields

Switches the display between field codes and field results, either for specific fields or for the entire document. Generally, you want to see field results in a document (the date itself), not field codes (the code that tells Word to insert the date). However, you can display the codes if you like; this technique is primarily useful if you're editing or formatting fields, or if you want to be able to easily spot all the fields in your document.

Certain fields—including index entries and table of contents entries—have hidden field codes. If you want to see these field codes, you need to display hidden text (see HIDDEN TEXT).

You can also decide whether to shade the fields in your documents:

1. Choose Tools, Options.
2. If necessary, click on the View tab.
3. Make a selection from under Field Shading.

Determines whether fields are never shaded, always shaded, or shaded when selected. If you're trying to track down a field, or need to be able to quickly pick out the fields in your document, the Always selection may be a good choice. If you find it difficult to distinguish between shaded fields and selected fields, however, you may want to turn shading off by selecting Never.

FIND AND REPLACE

See REPLACING TEXT, FORMATTING, AND SPECIAL CHARACTERS.

FINDING FILES

Word lets you hunt for files in specified drives and directories, search for files with specific names, look for files that contain particular summary information, and even find files that contain certain phrases or words. Once you've found a group of files, you can manage them in a variety of ways—opening, copying, printing, deleting, or sorting them.

Managing Files

1. Choose File, Find File.
2. If necessary, search for the desired group of files using the Search and/or Advanced Search dialog boxes (see "Searching for Files" later in this section).
3. Once the desired files are displayed under Listed Files, select the file or files to be affected.
4. Choose Open or choose Commands to select a command.

Enables you to open, copy, delete, or print one or more files. You can also sort all the listed files in a variety of ways, and can add or update summary information for a selected file. For specifics, see COPYING FILES, DELETING FILES, OPENING FILES, PRINTING, SORTING FILES, and SUMMARY INFO.

Don't become confused if, the first time you use Find File, Word takes you directly to the Search dialog box. It may do so if you've never searched for files. For details about how to proceed, see the upcoming section "Searching for Files."

If you want to operate on multiple files in the Find File dialog box, you must select them all first. To do so, click on the first file name to select it, and then hold down CTRL while clicking on the names of additional files to select them. To select multiple contiguous files, just drag over them; or else click to select one, hold down SHIFT, and then click to select a second file and all files in between. To deselect single selected files, hold down CTRL while clicking on them.

Saving Search Criteria

1. Specify search criteria in the Search and/or Advanced Search dialog boxes (see the next section, "Searching for Files").
2. When the desired search criteria are displayed under Search For in the Search dialog box, click on Save Search As.
3. Type a name for the search under Search Name.
4. Click on OK or press ENTER.

Saves the current search criteria so you can use them for future searches. Once you've saved a search, you can repeat it by selecting its name from the Saved Searches list box and clicking on OK. You can also delete a saved search by highlighting its name and pressing the Delete Search button.

Searching for Files

1. Choose File, Find File.
2. If you don't see the Search dialog box, choose the Search button in the Find File dialog box.
3. Specify a file name or file category under File Name.
4. Specify a drive and/or directory to be searched under Location. If you want to search all subdirectories of selected directories, select Include Subdirectories.
5. To specify additional search criteria, click on the Advanced Search button and make selections from the Advanced Search dialog box. Click on OK or press ENTER when you're done.
6. Click on OK or press ENTER in the Search dialog box to initiate the search.
7. Click on Close to clear the Find File dialog box when you're done viewing files.

Generates and then displays a list of files meeting the specified search criteria. When you open the Search dialog box, the search criteria from the previous search are still in place. You can remove all search criteria with the Clear button.

You can use wild cards when searching for file names. In the File Name text box (in either the Search dialog box or the Advanced Search dialog box), you can use * to specify any number of characters and ? to specify any one character. You can also specify multiple criteria by separating them with semicolons.

In the Advanced Search dialog box, you can choose the Location tab to search by location, the Summary tab to search according to the document's contents or summary information (see SUMMARY INFO), or the Timestamp tab to search for files saved or created on a specific date or range of dates. Note that you can use the Containing Text text box on the Summary tab to search for text within a document; this feature is invaluable if you can't

remember a document's name but can guess at some of
the text it contains. When you're done making selections
in all areas of the Advanced Search dialog box, click on
OK or press ENTER to return to the Search dialog box, and
again click on OK or press ENTER to initiate the search.

Viewing Files and File Information

When you select a file under Listed Files, by default you
see a preview of it on the right side of the Find File dialog
box. You can also choose File Info under View to see
basic information about the listed files—title, size, author,
and the date the file was last saved. Finally, you can
choose Summary under View to see summary information
for the highlighted file. If you want to enter or edit
summary information for a file, choose Commands,
Summary from the Find File dialog box (see SUMMARY
INFO).

You can choose whether to display the files contained in
the directories displayed under Listed Files. When a
directory's contents are displayed, a minus sign shows up
to the left of its directory icon. You can click on that
minus sign or double-click on the directory icon to remove
files from view, at which point the minus sign changes
into a plus sign. To bring files back into view, click on the
plus sign or double-click on the directory icon.

FINDING TEXT, FORMATTING, AND SPECIAL CHARACTERS

1. Choose Edit, Find.
2. Under Find What, type the text to be found.
3. Under Search, choose whether to search forward
   (Down), backward (Up), or through the entire document
   (All).
4. Click on Find Next or press ENTER to search for the
   designated text string.
5. Choose Cancel to close the Find dialog box when you're
   done with the search.

Keyboard Shortcuts:

CTRL+F   Displays the Find dialog box

SHIFT+F4   Repeats the previous Find command if the Find
            dialog box is closed

Finds the next instance of the specified text in the designated direction. You can search for further instances of the specified text item by repeatedly clicking on Find Next or pressing ENTER. If you've searched for several items during the current work session, they are listed in the Find What drop-down list box. To repeat a search, just pull down the list box and pick the item you want to search for.

If you want, you can search through only a portion of your document by selecting it before initiating the search. You can also refine your search by choosing the Match Case, Find Whole Words Only, Use Pattern Matching, and Sounds Like check boxes. If you select Match Case, Word only finds text strings that exactly match those that you enter under Find What. For example, if you enter tabouli under Find What and select Match Case, Word will find "tabouli" but not "TABOULI" or "Tabouli." And if you choose Find Whole Words Only, Word only finds complete words that match the text string. For example, if you enter her in the Find What text box and choose Find Whole Word Only, Word will find "her" but will not find "heresy," or "blather." If you select Use Pattern Matching, you can include special search operators in the Find What text box. For instance, you can use the ? operator to represent any single character, so a text string of c?t will find "cat," "cut," or "cot." Consult your Word documentation or the on-line help system for a list of all available search operators. If you select the Sounds Like check box, Word tracks down words that sound similar to the text string but are spelled differently.

You can also look for formatting and special characters. To search for formatting, choose the Format button in the Find dialog box. Then select Font to look for particular font characteristics, Paragraph to search for paragraph formatting, Language to track down text in a particular language, and Style to hunt for a specific style. Although you can look for a text string with the designated format, you can also search for a format alone by leaving the Find What box blank. To clear the selected formatting and begin a new search, choose the No Formatting button.

To look for special characters, choose the Special button and make a selection from the menu that appears. This inserts a special code representing the character in the

Find What text box; click on the Find Next button to search for that character.

Choosing the Replace button displays the Replace dialog box, in which you can find and then replace selected text strings, formatting, and special characters. (See REPLACING TEXT, FORMATTING, AND SPECIAL CHARACTERS for details.)

FONT

You can use a wide range of fonts—in a variety of styles and sizes—in your Word for Windows documents. In general, you can see the selected fonts, sizes, and font styles on the screen as you work, which makes it easy to judge the final appearance and impact of your document.

You can also apply a range of other character-based formatting, including text color, capitalization, character spacing, and more.

Changing Fonts and Font Attributes

1. Select the text to be altered.
2. Choose Format, Font.
3. If necessary, choose the Font tab.
4. Under Font, choose the desired font.
5. Under Font Style, choose the desired font attributes.
6. Under Size, choose a point size.
7. Click on OK or press ENTER.

Keyboard Shortcuts:

CTRL+]   Increases point size by one point

CTRL+[Decreases point size by one point

Mouse Shortcuts:

 Pull down this drop-down list to display a list of available fonts

 Pull down this drop-down list to display a list of available point sizes

Changes the font, font style, and size of the selected text. You can also use the Font dialog box to change text attributes such as text color, capitalization, underlining, and more. Select the Character Spacing tab if you wish to alter the spacing between characters (see SPACING).

Note that you can also change fonts as you type. Simply place the insertion point where you want the new font to begin, use any of the preceding methods to select a font, type the desired text, and then reverse your font selections when you're done.

To switch to a draft font so that your font selections don't show up on the screen, choose Options from the Tool menu, select the View tab, and then choose the Draft Font check box. To once again see your font selections on the screen, deselect the Draft Font check box. (This option is only available in Normal and Outline view.)

Copying Character Formatting

1. Select the text that includes the formatting to be copied.
2. Click on the Format Painter button (shown below) on the Standard toolbar.
3. Drag across the text to be formatted.

Keyboard Shortcuts:

CTRL+SHIFT+C   Copies character formatting of selected text
CTRL+SHIFT+V   Pastes the copied character formatting to selected text

Mouse Shortcut:

   Formats the text you drag across, using the formatting of the selected text

Copies all character-based formatting—including font and point size—from the text you selected initially to the text that you drag across. When you click on the Format Painter button, the mouse pointer changes into an I-beam and a paint brush to indicate that formatting will be "painted" onto text that you now select. When you release the mouse button, the pointer returns to normal. If you instead double-click on the Format Painter button, the mouse pointer remains a paint brush until you click on the Format Painter button again. This enables you to "paint" several areas of text using the specified format.

Establishing a New Default Font

1. Choose Format, Font.
2. Select the desired font characteristics.

3. Choose the Default button.

4. Choose Yes or press ENTER when asked whether to change the default font.

Changes the default font for the current template. When you use this template in the future, the new font settings will be in effect. (A *template* is a basic document design that determines not only the fonts but also the margins, spacing, and other formatting characteristics of documents that you create using the template.) Word for Windows uses the Normal template by default. If you change the font for this template, the new font will be in effect in the blank document that Word opens automatically when you load the program; in documents that you create using the New button on the Standard toolbar; and in documents that you create by choosing File, New and selecting Normal under Template. (See NEW FILE, TEMPLATES.)

You can also change the default font for the current template by selecting text that has the desired font characteristics. Then choose Format, Font, and choose Default.

Removing Character Formatting

1. Select the text whose formatting you wish to remove.

2. Press CTRL+SPACEBAR.

Removes all character formatting—including font, font style, and point size—from the selected text, so that the selected text has only the characteristics stipulated under the default font style for the current template.

FOOTERS

See HEADERS AND FOOTERS.

FOOTNOTES AND ENDNOTES

Word for Windows makes it easy to create footnotes, endnotes, or both in order to include explanatory text or references that don't belong in the main body of your document. When you add a note to your document, you're really adding two items: a reference mark within the text, and the note itself. Footnotes appear on the same page as their reference mark, while endnotes appear at either the end of the section or the end of the document.

Adding Notes

1. Place the insertion point where you want the footnote or endnote reference mark to appear.
2. Choose Insert, Footnote.
3. Choose either Footnote or Endnote.
4. Click on OK or press ENTER.
5. Type the footnote or endnote text.
6. If you're in Normal view, choose Close when you're done typing the note text.

Keyboard Shortcuts:

ALT+CTRL+F   Inserts a footnote

ALT+CTRL+E   Inserts an endnote

Enables you to include footnotes or endnotes with your documents. If you're in Normal view, a note pane opens and you type footnote and endnote text there. If you're in Page Layout view, you type the note text in its actual location in the document.

Notes that you add are numbered automatically if you leave the AutoNumber option in the Footnote and Endnote dialog box selected. You can also choose Custom Mark and enter a custom reference mark of up to ten characters in the Custom Mark text box. Or, you can click on Symbol to create a custom mark from the various character sets available in the Symbol dialog box.

Choosing Options in the Footnote and Endnote dialog box lets you further customize the numbering and placement of notes. You can use the Convert button in the Note Options dialog box to change footnotes to endnotes and vice versa (see "Converting Notes").

Converting Notes

To convert selected notes:

1. If necessary, choose View, Normal to switch to Normal view.
2. Choose View, Footnotes.

3. If necessary, choose All Footnotes or All Endnotes from the view drop-down list box at the top of the note pane to choose the desired type of notes.

4. In the note pane, select the notes to be converted.

5. Click the right mouse button within the note pane to display the shortcut menu for notes.

6. Choose Convert to Footnote or Convert to Endnote.

To convert all notes:

1. Choose Insert, Footnote.

2. Choose Options and then choose either the All Footnotes or the All Endnotes tab.

3. Choose the Convert button.

4. Select the desired conversion option and then click on OK or press ENTER.

5. Click on OK or press ENTER until you return to your document.

Converts the designated footnotes into endnotes, or vice versa. You can even change footnotes to endnotes and endnotes to footnotes in a single operation with the Swap Footnotes and Endnotes button.

Copying and Moving Notes

1. Select the note's reference mark in the text.

2. Drag the reference mark to a new location to move the note. Hold down the CTRL key while dragging the reference mark to copy the note.

3. Release the mouse button to deposit the note in its new spot.

Moves or copies the note to a new location in your document. In either case, Word renumbers notes as necessary to keep footnote and endnote numbers in sequence. You can also cut or copy and then paste to move and copy notes (see CUT AND PASTE and COPYING TEXT AND GRAPHICS). And if you move or copy blocks of text that contain note reference marks, any reference marks included will be moved or copied and renumbered accordingly.

Deleting Notes

1. Within the text, select the reference mark of the note to be deleted.

2. Press BACKSPACE or DEL.

Deletes the selected footnote or endnote, automatically renumbering any subsequent notes. You cannot delete notes by deleting the note text, either in the note pane or in Page Layout view. This removes the note text but not the note itself. If you delete a block of text that contains notes, the notes are deleted and any subsequent notes are renumbered as necessary.

Viewing Notes

1. Choose View, Footnotes if notes are not already displayed.

Mouse Shortcut:

Double-click on note's reference mark in text	Moves insertion point to note in question, opening note pane if you're in Normal view
Double-click on reference mark to left of note itself	Moves insertion point to note's reference mark in text, closing note pane if you're in Normal view

Displays all the footnotes or endnotes in the active document. In Normal view, opens the note pane and displays either footnotes or endnotes. If your document contains both note types, you can choose All Endnotes or All Footnotes in the view drop-down list box at the top of the note pane to switch between viewing footnotes and viewing endnotes. In Page Layout view, choosing View, Footnotes displays the View Footnotes dialog box, from which you can choose to view either the Footnote area or the Endnote area.

To return to your document, you can click on the note pane's Close button in Normal view. Or you can click within your document or press F6 to return to your document without closing the note pane. You can also use Word's Go To feature to move to the reference mark of a specific note within the text (see GO TO).

FORMS

You can create forms to be filled out by hand simply by leaving blank areas in your text or blank table cells that can be filled in with information. In addition, you can create special forms—either text-based or table-based—that can be filled in on line. These on-line forms are similar to other forms you might create, but also make use of *form fields*: special areas that the user fills in either by typing in text, checking or unchecking check boxes, or choosing options from drop-down list boxes.

When you construct forms that are to be used on line, you should create a document template rather than a regular document file—this ensures that all relevant macros and AutoText entries will be available when the form is being filled in. (A *template* is essentially a document blueprint that can include text, formatting, styles, macros, graphics, and more.) Word includes several form templates that you can use or modify; in addition, you can create your own form templates from scratch (see TEMPLATES). On-line forms also must be protected before the form fields are activated; this way users can only make entries or selections in the form fields, and cannot unintentionally change the form itself (see PROTECTING DOCUMENTS).

Building On-Line Forms

1. Choose File, New. (In this case, don't use the New button on the Standard toolbar.)
2. Select Template under New, and click on OK or press ENTER to create a new template based on the Normal template, Word's default template.
3. Create your form using any table and formatting features.
4. Place the insertion point where you want users to be able to enter information or select choices.
5. Choose Insert, Form Field.
6. Select the type of form field to insert (Text, Check Box, or Drop-Down).
7. To further define the characteristics of the form field, choose Options and make selections from the Options dialog box that appears, choosing OK or pressing ENTER when you're done.
8. Repeat steps 4 through 7 to add additional form fields to your form.
9. Choose Tools, Protect Document.
10. Choose Forms, and click on OK or press ENTER.

11. Choose File, Save and name the form. (Word adds the .DOT extension automatically and saves the template in the TEMPLATE subdirectory.)

12. Choose File, Close.

Mouse Shortcuts:

ab|	Inserts text form field
⊠	Inserts check box form field
▤	Inserts drop-down form field
▦	Protects (or unprotects) the active document

Creates a form that the user can fill in on line by making entries and selections in special form fields. The Forms toolbar—use View, Toolbars or the Show Toolbar button in the Form Field dialog box—provides convenient shortcuts for creating, modifying, and protecting on-line forms.

Text form fields are for entering numbers or items of text that will vary, including addresses, dates, and so on. Check box form fields are primarily for yes/no or true/false answers, such as Male or Female. Drop-down form fields permit you to provide users with a list of choices from which to choose—such as Freshman, Sophomore, Junior, and Senior.

Filling in On-Line Forms

1. Choose File, New. (Don't use the New button on the Standard toolbar as a shortcut in this case.)

2. Choose the desired form template under Template, make sure Document is selected under New, and then click on OK or press ENTER.

3. When the new document opens on your screen, the first form field is automatically selected. Enter text or make a selection and press ENTER to move to the next form field, continuing until you're done filling out the form.

4. Choose File, Save As.

5. Under File Name, enter a name for the filled-in copy of the form.

6. Click on OK or press ENTER.

Produces a filled-in copy of the selected on-line form. Note that, in addition to moving between form fields by pressing ENTER, you can move between them by clicking on them, pressing TAB (to go to the next field), SHIFT+TAB (to go to the previous field), or the arrow keys.

Modifying On-Line Forms

1. Choose File, Open.
2. Select Document Templates under List Files of Type.
3. Choose the desired template from the File Name list box and then click on OK or press ENTER. (You may need to switch to the TEMPLATE directory to find the template you want.)
4. Choose Tools, Unprotect Document.
5. To modify form fields, double-click on them and make selections from the Form Field Options dialog box.
6. To add form fields, place the insertion point in the desired location and choose Insert, Form Field.
7. To add text to your form or edit existing text, just use normal editing techniques.
8. When you're done, choose Tools, Protect Document.
9. Choose File, Save.

Mouse Shortcuts:

 Unprotects protected documents, or protects unprotected documents

 Enables you to change options for the selected form field

Modifies the form template for the selected on-line form. See "Building On-Line Forms" for details on the different types of form fields available.

FRAMES

A *frame* is like a receptacle in which you can insert text, graphics, tables, and other objects in order to position them more easily and more precisely within your document. You can place framed objects anywhere on the page, and can also easily change the size of the frame. When you work with frames, you will probably want to switch to Page Layout view so that you can see the frame's exact location on the page and use dragging techniques to move and change the size of the frame.

Most frames do not print when you print your document. (The exception is that, when you frame text, Word automatically places a border around it.) To place a printing border around a table, a graphic, or any other object, use the borders feature (see BORDERS).

Inserting Frames

To frame an existing object:

1. If necessary, switch to Page Layout view and then select the object.
2. Choose Insert, Frame.

To insert an empty frame:

1. If necessary, switch to Page Layout view and make sure no objects are selected.
2. Choose Insert, Frame.
3. Drag the crosshair pointer to mark out the frame size.
4. When the dotted outline is of the desired size, release the mouse pointer.

Mouse Shortcut:

 Insert Frame button on Forms toolbar; frames selected item or inserts an empty frame

Frames the selected object or inserts an empty frame of the designated size. If you insert a frame around an existing object, the frame size is tailored to fit that object. When you insert a frame around text, the frame is automatically given a line border; to apply borders to other objects such as graphics, see BORDERS.

Positioning Frames

1. Select the frame to be moved.
2. Choose Format, Frame.
3. Under both Horizontal and Vertical, make selections for Position and Relative To.
4. When you're done, click on OK or press ENTER.

Mouse Shortcuts:

Drag frame (*not* sizing handles), releasing mouse button when dashed outline is in desired location

Repositions selected frame (don't drag on the sizing handles or you'll change the frame size)

Repositions the selected frame. If you drag to move the
frame, you position it by eye and release the mouse
button to drop it in the selected location. If you use the
Frame dialog box, however, you can position the frame
relative to the page, the margin, the column, or the
paragraph.

When you add and delete text, the frame remains in the
designated position on the page, unless you select the
Move With Text check box in the Frame dialog box. You
can also stipulate that a frame remains with a designated
paragraph by selecting the Lock Anchor check box, which
locks the frame to the nearest paragraph. (Consult your
Word documentation or the on-line help system for
details on anchoring.)

Removing Frames

1. Make sure you're in Page Layout view.
2. Select the frame to be deleted.
3. Choose Format, Frame.
4. Choose Remove Frame.

Removes the frame from around the selected object. You
can also delete a frame along with its contents by
selecting the frame (in Page Layout view) and then
pressing BACKSPACE or DEL.

Selecting Frames

1. Switch to Page Layout view.
2. Position the mouse pointer over the frame.
3. When the mouse pointer becomes a positioning pointer
   (an arrow with a four-headed arrow attached), click to
   select the frame.

Selects the frame you clicked on, enclosing it within a
crosshatched border plus eight small square sizing
handles (one on each corner and one on each side), or
two sizing handles, (one each side) in the case of tables.
You must select frames before you can manipulate them
in any way.

Sizing Frames

1. Select the frame.
2. Choose Format, Frame.

3. Select Exactly from the Width drop-down list box and type or select a value in the At text box.

4. Select Exactly from the Height drop-down list box and type or select a value in the At text box.

5. Click on OK or press ENTER.

Mouse Shortcut:

Drag sizing handle, releasing mouse button when dashed outline is of desired size	Increases or decreases size of selected frame; drag on a corner handle to change the size of two sides at once

Changes the size of the selected frame. Note that if you use the dragging technique and the frame and graphic are of the same size, this increases or decreases the size of the graphic within its frame. (You can change the frame size alone by using the Frame dialog box.) It does not, however, change the size of text; it just changes the size of the frame enclosing the text, and may cause the text to rewrap to accommodate the new frame.

Wrapping Text Around Frames

1. Switch to Page Layout view and select the frame in question.

2. Choose Format, Frame.

3. Select Around under Text Wrapping.

4. Click on OK or press ENTER.

Allows text to wrap around the selected frame, instead of stopping where the frame begins and resuming where it ends. You can also set the distance between the frame and the surrounding text by choosing Distance from Text under Horizontal and specifying the distance between the frame and the text to its left and right, and by choosing Distance from Text under Vertical and specifying the distance between the frame and the text above and below it.

FULL SCREEN

See "The Different Views" under "General Procedures."

GO TO

1. Choose <u>E</u>dit, <u>G</u>o To.
2. Under Go to <u>W</u>hat, select the type of item to go to.
3. Choose Nex<u>t</u> or <u>P</u>revious to go to the next or previous instance of the selected item; or, enter the name or number of the specific item you want to go to in the <u>E</u>nter box and click on Go <u>T</u>o.
4. When you've found the desired item, click on Close to close the Go To dialog box.

Keyboard Shortcut:

F5 or CTRL+G   Opens the Go To dialog box

Mouse Shortcut:

Double-click the page   Opens the Go To dialog box
number in the lower-left
corner of screen

Moves the insertion point to the page, section, bookmark, note, or other selected item in question. In the Go To dialog box, you can also enter + (plus sign) followed by a number and select Go <u>T</u>o to move forward the designated number of items relative to your current position, and you can enter − (minus sign) followed by a number and select Go <u>T</u>o to move backward the designated number of items relative to your current position.

GRAMMAR CHECKING

1. Choose <u>T</u>ools, <u>G</u>rammar.
2. Respond to the suggestions in the Spelling and Grammar dialog boxes.
3. If you like, scan the Readability Statistics dialog box that appears when the grammar check is done.
4. Choose OK to return to your document.

Causes Word to check the current document for grammatical errors, spelling mistakes, or stylistic glitches. When the grammar check is completed, Word displays a series of "readability statistics." Note that you can check just a portion of your document by selecting it before initiating the grammar check.

In the Grammar dialog box, you can click on the Change button to accept the suggested change or you can edit the text under Sentence. You can also click on the Ignore button to bypass the current suggestion, or you can click on the Ignore Rule button to disregard the rule in question for the remainder of the grammar check under way. If you like, select Explain to read a description of the grammatical rule being applied. Choose Next Sentence to move directly to the next sentence, without checking the current sentence any further. Choose Undo Last to reverse the most recent correction, and, as you'd expect, choose Cancel to halt the grammar check in midstream. Finally, choose Options if you want to customize how the grammar check takes place. (See "Grammar" under OPTIONS.)

GRAPHICS

You can draw directly in Word using the Drawing toolbar, and you can import art created in other applications by using Windows cut and paste features or by using the Picture command on the Insert menu. Although creating or importing graphics is beyond the scope of this book, this section briefly describes some ways in which you can manipulate graphics that you've either created in Word or imported into Word from another source.

You need to select graphics before you can manipulate them in any way. With a mouse, you can select a graphic just by clicking on it; this introduces a border and eight square handles around the graphic. (Be sure to click *only once* on a graphic to select it: clicking twice may open the application in which the graphic was created.) To select graphics with the keyboard, place the insertion point just before the graphic and press SHIFT+RIGHT ARROW.

You can enclose graphics in frames to more easily position them on the screen (see FRAMES). You can also apply borders, but not shading, to graphics. Also see COPYING TEXT AND GRAPHICS, DELETING TEXT AND GRAPHICS, EMBEDDING, and LINKING.

Cropping Graphics

1. Select the graphic to be cropped.

2. Hold down SHIFT as you drag one of the handles in toward the graphic.

3. Release the mouse button when the dashed outline is enclosing the desired portion of the graphic.

Crops the selected graphic as indicated. This changes which portion of the image you see, without (as with sizing) changing the proportions of the overall image. As you drag, the mouse pointer changes into a special cropping symbol and cropping measurements show up at the bottom of the screen. As when sizing images, you can drag on a corner handle to crop on two sides at once; dragging on a side handle just crops one side of the image at a time. You can also add white space around a graphic by "cropping" outward from the image.

You can employ the Picture command on the Format menu to crop images. To do so, just make selections under Crop From in the Picture dialog box. Enter negative values if you want to add white space around the image rather than removing a portion of it from view.

Inserting Graphics

1. Place the insertion point in the desired location.

2. Choose Insert, Picture.

3. Select the name of a graphic file under File Name. If necessary, change file specifications, drives, and/or directories to find the desired file.

4. Select the Preview Picture check box if you want to see a preview of the image.

5. Click on OK or press ENTER.

Places the graphic in your document at the insertion point. You can also import graphics from other Windows applications by using standard Windows cutting (or copying) and pasting techniques (see CUT AND PASTE).

Moving Graphics

1. If necessary, switch to Page Layout view.

2. Use Insert, Frame to frame the graphic if it isn't already framed.

3. Select the graphic, place the mouse pointer within it (the pointer will change into a positioning pointer, an arrow with a four-headed arrow attached), and drag to move the graphic to a new spot.

4. Release the mouse button when the dashed rectangular outline is in the desired location.

Moves the selected graphic to the location indicated by the dashed rectangular outline. Make sure to avoid the sizing handles when you drag, or you'll wind up resizing rather than relocating the graphic. Although you can move graphics without enclosing them within a frame, framing enables you to move them much more easily and with more precision (see FRAMES).

Restoring Graphics

1. Select the desired graphic.
2. Choose Format, Picture.
3. Click on the Reset button, and then click on OK or press ENTER.

Mouse Shortcut:

CTRL+double-click   Reverses any resizing or cropping to an imported graphic

Returns the selected graphic to its original size and reverses any cropping. Use this command if you resize a graphic and realize you've distorted it, or if you decide to reverse any cropping you've done.

Sizing Graphics

1. Select the desired graphic.
2. Place the mouse pointer over a handle (the pointer should change into double-headed arrow).
3. Drag to change the size of the graphic.
4. Release the mouse button when the dashed rectangular outline is of the desired size.

Changes the size of the selected graphic. As you drag, a dashed outline indicates the new size the graphic will take on if you release the mouse button. If you drag on a middle handle, the graphic changes size in that direction only, and does not retain its original proportions. If you drag on a corner handle, the graphic is resized proportionally. As you drag, the status bar indicates the graphic's percentage of its original height and width.

You can also use the Format, Picture command to change the size of a selected graphic. In the Picture dialog box, make selections under Size to establish an exact width and height for the graphic. Or, under Scaling, increase or decrease the size of the graphic in relative terms.

GRAPHS

Word for Windows includes a special program, Microsoft Graph, that enables you to create graphs and insert them into your documents. Note that you can graph existing tables of data, or you can get into Microsoft Graph and then enter data to be graphed. To open Microsoft Graph, choose Insert, Object, choose the Create New tab, if necessary, select Microsoft Graph from the Object Type list, and then click on OK or press ENTER. An in-depth discussion of Microsoft Graph is beyond the scope of this book.

Mouse Shortcut:

   Opens Microsoft Graph

HEADERS AND FOOTERS

Headers and footers are repeating text that you generally include in the top (headers) or bottom (footers) margin of every page of your document. Headers and footers typically include identifying information such as the document title, the page number, and the chapter number. They can also include longer amounts of text, fields, and even graphics.

Creating Headers and Footers

1. Choose View, Header and Footer.
2. Enter text for the header or footer in the Header and Footer areas that open.
3. If necessary, switch between the header and footer areas by scrolling or by using the Switch Between Header and Footer button.
4. When you're done, click on the Close button on the Header and Footer toolbar or double-click on the grayed document area.

Mouse Shortcuts:

   Switches between Header area and Footer area

Inserts page number field

 Inserts date field

 Inserts time field

Grays the bulk of your document, opens the Header and Footer areas, and displays the Header and Footer toolbar—enabling you to add headers and/or footers to the active document. It does not matter which page you are on when you initiate this process if you're entering a header or footer that is to be used for the entire document. Once you close the Header and Footer areas, headers and footers do not show up in Normal view. In Page Layout view, they show up as grayed text at the top and/or bottom of the page.

You can add fields to headers and footers. The page number, date, and time buttons on the Header and Footer toolbar add fields automatically. In addition, you can add other fields manually by using the Insert, Field command—for example, you could add a field to insert the file name in the header (see FIELDS).

Deleting Headers and Footers

1. Choose View, Header and Footer.
2. Select all text and fields in the desired header or footer and press BACKSPACE or DEL.
3. Choose Close or double-click in the grayed document text to return to your document.

Deletes the selected header or footer. If your document consists of just one section, or if you have not created different headers and footers for the different sections in your document, this deletes all headers and/or footers. If your document consists of multiple sections that contain different headers and/or footers, you must go to each section and delete its header or footer separately (see "Varying Headers and Footers").

Editing Headers and Footers

1. Choose View, Header and Footer.
2. Edit or format the header or footer text and fields.

3. If necessary, scroll or use the Switch Between Header and Footer button to move between the header and footer text.

4. When you're done, click on Close in the Header and Footer toolbar.

Mouse Shortcuts:

In Page Layout view, double-click on the grayed header or footer text within the document	Opens the Header or Footer area and the Header and Footer toolbar
Double-click on the grayed document text when the Header and Footer areas are open	Closes the Header and Footer areas, closes the Header and Footer toolbar, and returns you to the view you were in when you opened the Header and Footer areas

Changes the headers and/or footers for the entire document if your document consists of just one section or if you have not created different headers and footers for different sections. Otherwise, this changes only the specific headers or footers you edited. To change any other headers or footers, move to them and modify them as well.

Varying Headers and Footers

To create a different header and/or footer for the first page of a document:

1. Choose View, Header and Footer.

2. Choose File, Page Setup.

3. If necessary, choose the Layout tab.

4. Under Headers and Footers, select the Different First Page check box and click on OK or press ENTER.

5. Move to the Header or Footer area on the first page (it will be labeled First Page Header or First Page Footer) and create the desired header or footer (leave the area blank to suppress headers and/or footers for the first page).

6. If necessary, go to the Header or Footer area on a subsequent page and then create headers and/or footers for the rest of the document.

7. Click on Close to return to your document.

To create different headers and/or footers for odd and even pages:

1. Choose <u>V</u>iew, <u>H</u>eader and Footer.
2. Choose <u>F</u>ile, Page Set<u>up</u>.
3. If necessary, choose the <u>L</u>ayout tab.
4. Under Headers and Footers, select the Different <u>O</u>dd and Even check box and click on OK or press ENTER.
5. Move to a header or footer on an even page (it will be labeled Even Page Header or Even Page Footer) and enter the text for even headers and footers.
6. Move to a header or footer on an odd page and enter the text for odd headers and footers.
7. Choose the <u>C</u>lose button to return to your document.

To create different headers and/or footers for different sections of your document:

1. Move to a section in which you want different headers and footers than in the preceding section.
2. Choose <u>V</u>iew, <u>H</u>eader and Footer to display the Header and Footer areas (they will be labeled with the section number).
3. Click on the Same as Previous button on the Header and Footer toolbar to deselect it.
4. Create the desired headers and footers; you can either modify old ones or create entirely new ones.
5. Click on the <u>C</u>lose button to return to your document.

Mouse Shortcuts:

 Opens the Page Setup dialog box

 Same as Previous button; when deselected, enables you to create different headers and footers in different sections

 Show Previous button; enables you to move between the sections in your document to create varying headers and/or footers

 Show Ne<u>x</u>t button; enables you to move between the sections in your document to create varying headers and/or footers

Enables you to establish different headers and footers in different areas of your document. Even if your document consists of multiple sections, any headers and footers apply throughout by default. However, you can "disconnect" a section from the previous ones by deselecting the Same as Previous button on the Header and Footer toolbar. Unlinking a section in this way permits you to create new headers or footers within it. All subsequent sections now take on the new headers or footers, unless you unlink them from the previous section as well, as just described.

You can also relink sections so that they once again have the same headers and/or footers:

1. Place the insertion point in the section whose headers or footers you want to resemble the headers or footers in the preceding section.

2. Choose View, Header and Footer.

3. Click on the Same as Previous button on the Header and Footer toolbar to select it (it should look pushed in).

4. Respond Yes when asked whether you want to connect the current headers/footers to those of the previous section.

5. Click on the Close button in the Header and Footer toolbar or double-click on the grayed document text to return to your document.

HELP SYSTEM

See "When You Need Help" under "General Procedures."

HIDDEN TEXT

1. Select the desired text.

2. Choose Format, Font.

3. If necessary, choose the Font tab.

4. Under Effects, select the Hidden check box.

5. Click on OK or press ENTER.

Keyboard Shortcut:

CTRL+SHIFT+H   Changes selected text to hidden text, or if
                hidden text is displayed on screen, changes
                hidden text to regular text or vice versa

Mouse Shortcut:

 Reveals or conceals all nonprinting characters

Changes the selected text to hidden text, which will not
be displayed when printed. Hidden text may or may not
show up on your screen. By default, it does not. You can
reveal hidden text—as well as a variety of other
nonprinting characters such as paragraph marks and tab
characters—with the Show/Hide button on the Standard
toolbar (shown above). The hidden text will show up on
screen as text with dotted underlining.

HYPHENATION

Word for Windows enables you to control the flow of text
in your documents by using hyphenation to break words
at the end of each line of text. This can improve the
appearance of left-aligned text that has a very ragged
right margin, and can also remove unsightly gaps
between words in justified documents.

Automatic Hyphenation

1. If you don't want to hyphenate the entire document,
   select the text to be hyphenated.
2. Choose Tools, Hyphenation.
3. Select the check box Automatically Hyphenate
   Document.
4. Click on OK or press ENTER.

Hyphenates your document (or the selected text)
automatically using the specifications in the Hyphenation
dialog box.

By default, Word will hyphenate capitalized words. To
prevent it from doing so, choose the Hyphenate Words in
CAPS check box to deselect it. You can also specify a
value in the Limit Consecutive Hyphens To check box to
restrict the number of consecutive lines of text that end
in hyphens.

The *hyphenation zone* is the maximum amount of space
permitted between the end of the last word on the line
and right margin. A wider hyphenation zone yields fewer
hyphens, while a narrow zone produces more hyphens. If

necessary, adjust this zone to reduce or increase the number of hyphens in your document.

If you want Word to refrain from hyphenating a portion of your document, select the text in question, choose Format, Paragraph, click on the Text Flow tab if necessary, select the Don't Hyphenate check box, and click on OK or press ENTER.

Manual Hyphenation

1. If you don't want to hyphenate the entire document, select the text to be hyphenated.
2. Choose Tools, Hyphenation and choose Manual.
3. In the Manual Hyphenation dialog box, choose Yes to insert the suggested hyphen (indicated by a flashing selection bar); or click where you want to insert a hyphen and then choose Yes; or choose No to prohibit Word from hyphenating the current word.
4. Repeat this procedure for any other word that Word for Windows suggests you hyphenate.
5. Click on OK or press ENTER when Word informs you that hyphenation is complete.

Enables you to place hyphens where you want them. Word displays the Manual Hyphenation dialog box each time it suggests that a word be hyphenated. As with automatic hyphenation, you can select areas of your document to shield them from hyphenation.

Using Nonbreaking Hyphens

1. Place the insertion point where you want to insert a hyphen that will not break.
2. Press CTRL+SHIFT+HYPHEN.

Inserts a *nonbreaking hyphen,* which ensures that a hyphenated compound word does not break at the end of a line. This is especially useful with names.

Using Optional Hyphens

1. Place the insertion point where you want to insert an optional hyphen.
2. Press CTRL+HYPHEN.

Specifies where you want Word to hyphenate a word if it needs to be broken at the end of a line. (These are the kinds of hyphens that Word inserts when you have it hyphenate your document for you.) Optional hyphens only show up if necessary. If you edit your document, text rewraps, and a word containing an optional hyphen no longer needs to be hyphenated, the hyphen is removed from view.

INDENTATION

1. Place the insertion point within the paragraph to be changed, or select the paragraphs to be changed.
2. Choose F_o_rmat, _P_aragraph.
3. If necessary, choose the _I_ndents and Spacing tab.
4. Choose _L_eft and specify a value to determine how far text is indented from the left margin.
5. Choose _R_ight and specify a value to determine how far text is indented from the right margin.
6. If you want to set a hanging indent or a first-line indent, make the desired selection under _S_pecial and specify the amount of the indent under B_y_.
7. When you're done, click on OK or press ENTER.

Keyboard Shortcuts:

CTRL+M	Increases left paragraph indent one tab stop
CTRL+SHIFT+M	Decreases left paragraph indent one tab stop
CTRL+SHIFT+N	Removes indents by applying the Normal style
CTRL+T	Creates hanging indent
CTRL+SHIFT+T	Removes hanging indent

Mouse Shortcuts:

 Indents paragraph(s) to previous tab stop

 Indents paragraph(s) to next tab stop

Changes the location of the left, right, and first-line indents—in other words, determines where text begins in relation to the margins. Setting the left and right indents generally moves text toward or away from the margins in tab stop increments. You can also create negative left or right indents to move text into the margins. In addition, you can set a *first-line indent* to have the first line of every selected paragraph indented relative to the left indent. Finally, you can create *hanging indents*, where the first line of text extends to the left of the rest of the paragraph.

If you prefer using the mouse, you can change the indents by dragging on the left indent, right indent, and first-line indent markers on the ruler. (The left indent marker is an upward-pointing triangle on top of a square on the left edge of the ruler by default. The right indent marker is an upward-pointing triangle on the right edge of the ruler by default. The first-line indent marker is a downward-pointing triangle at the left edge of the ruler by default.) Simply drag these markers to the desired location to change the indentation of the current paragraph or of selected paragraphs. To create a hanging indent, just place the left indent marker to the right of the first-line indent marker. Note that when you drag the left indent marker's triangle, you move the left indent alone, whereas if you drag its square, you move the left indent as well as the first-line indent.

INDEXES

As you probably know, an *index* consists of an alphabetical list of topics—usually at the end of the document—along with page numbers listing where those topics appear in the text. Word makes it surprisingly easy to construct an index. The two basic steps are first to mark index entries within the text, and then to compile the index and choose where to place it in your document.

If you're indexing a long manuscript, you may want to make use of the master document feature (see MASTER DOCUMENTS). This would enable you to create a book consisting of separate chapters, for example, but to index the entire book as a single document. You can also index automatically by first creating a concordance file listing the entries to be included in the index. For more on the

ins and outs of indexing, you may want to consult your
Word documentation or the on-line help system.

Compiling an Index

1. Mark all the desired index entries, as described under
   "Marking Index Entries" later in this section.

2. Place the insertion point where you want the index to
   go.

3. Choose Insert, Index and Tables.

4. If necessary, click on the Index tab.

5. Select the desired index format under Formats (look
   under Preview for a sample).

6. Click on OK or press ENTER to generate the index.

Using the marked index entries, generates an index in
the designated location in your document. Word
automatically inserts section breaks before and after the
index, tracks down and alphabetizes all the marked index
entries, and follows each entry with a page number or
range of pages. The index that Word generates is actually
a field; this enables you to update it easily if and when
there are changes to your manuscript.

Under Type in the Index and Tables dialog box, you can
choose whether you want subentries below the main
entry and indented (Indented) or on the same line as the
associated main entry (Run-in). (A subentry would be
something like "Compiling" under "Indexes.") You can also
decide how many columns to use for your index, and
whether to right align page numbers. If you right align
page numbers, you can insert a tab leader (such as a
dashed or dotted line) between the entry and the page
number.

Marking Index Entries

1. Select the text to be used as an index entry.

2. Choose Insert, Index and Tables.

3. If necessary, click on the Index tab.

4. Click on Mark Entry.

5. In the Mark Index Entry dialog box, enter text or edit
   the text entry under Main Entry if necessary.

6. Click on the <u>M</u>ark button; or click on Mark <u>A</u>ll to mark every instance of the selected text that exactly matches the case of the entry under Main <u>E</u>ntry.

7. Scroll through your document and mark additional text entries as described in steps 1 through 6.

8. Click on Close or press ENTER to close the Mark Index Entry dialog box when you're done marking entries.

Keyboard Shortcut:

ALT+SHIFT+X   Opens the Mark Index Entry dialog box

Marks entries that are to be included in the index. Once you've marked all the desired entries, you are ready to compile the index.

In the Mark Index Entry dialog box, you can type subentries under <u>S</u>ubentry, and can even include multiple subentries by separating them by colons. You can also create cross-references to other topics in the index; select <u>C</u>ross-reference and type the reference text after *See*. In addition, you can specify a range of pages instead of a specific page for a particular entry by selecting Page <u>R</u>ange and selecting the desired bookmark. (You must first mark the page range with a bookmark; see BOOKMARKS.)

Updating Indexes

1. Choose <u>I</u>nsert, Inde<u>x</u> and Tables.

2. If necessary, click on the Inde<u>x</u> tab; then click on OK or press ENTER.

3. Select <u>Y</u>es when asked whether to replace the selected index.

Mouse Shortcut:

Place the insertion point anywhere within the index and press F9   Updates the index

Recompiles the index associated with the current document. You may need to do this if the document changes and marked index entries move to different pages, or if you mark additional index entries. In addition, you can update an index to change its format.

INSERTING FILES

1. Place the insertion point where you want to insert the file.
2. Choose Insert, File.
3. Under File Name, enter the name of the file to be inserted. (If necessary, switch drives and/or directories, or choose a different file type under List Files of Type, to find the file.)
4. Click on OK or press ENTER.

Inserts the complete text of the designated file into your document at the insertion point. Normally, this inserts just the document text. However, if you select the Link to File check box in the File dialog box, Word instead inserts a field code representing the document. Then when the original document changes, you can update the code and the changes to the original will be reflected. (See FIELDS and LINKING.)

You can specify that you only want to insert a selected portion of the document by entering a bookmark name or a named range under Range (see BOOKMARKS).

INSERT MODE

1. Press the INS key or double-click on the OVR indicator at the bottom of the screen.

Turns on insert mode, if it's not already on; turns it off if it's on. (You know insert mode is on if the OVR indicator is grayed.) In insert mode, text that you type pushes existing text to the right instead of overwriting it. (Insert mode is on by default.)

Note that you can customize Word so that you can use the INS key instead of CTRL+V to paste the contents of the Clipboard into your document, in which case INS does not toggle insert mode on and off. See "Edit" under OPTIONS for details. Also refer to OVERTYPE MODE.

ITALIC

To italicize existing text:

1. Select the text to be italicized.
2. Choose Format, Font and click on the Font tab if necessary.
3. Choose Italic under Font Style.
4. Click on OK or press ENTER.

To italicize text as you type

1. Place the insertion point where you want to type italic text.
2. Choose Format, Font and click on the Font tab if necessary.
3. Choose Italic under Font Style.
4. Click on OK or press ENTER.
5. Type the desired text.
6. Choose Format, Font.
7. Choose Regular under Font Style.
8. Click on OK or press ENTER.

Keyboard Shortcut:

CTRL+I   Italicizes the selected text or the text you type (turns off italic if it's already on)

Mouse Shortcut:

    Italicizes the selected text or the text you type (turns off italic if it's already on)

Creates characters that are slanted to the right. Italic is often used to set off terms that are being defined and to accentuate headings.

JUSTIFICATION

See ALIGNMENT.

LABELS

1. Choose Tools, Envelopes and Labels.

2. If necessary, click on the Labels tab.

3. Under Address, enter an address for the recipient if necessary.

4. To include a return address, select Use Return Address and, if necessary, enter a return address.

5. Under Print, choose Full Page of the Same Label; or, choose Single Label and make selections under Row and Column to determine the label's location.

6. Click on Print.

Prints a single label or an entire sheet of labels containing the same information. (Printing different labels is discussed under MAIL MERGE.) If you select text before initiating the labels command, Word uses that text as the recipient's address. Otherwise, Word guesses which text is the address; you can edit this selection. If you select Use Return Address, Word automatically inserts the return address listed under User Info (see OPTIONS). You can either accept, edit, or replace this address.

If you need to select a new label size or change any printing options, choose Options in the Envelopes and Labels dialog box. Make the desired selections in the Label Options dialog box; if you like, click on Details to see the precise specifications for the label type you select under Product Number; you can also make modifications to the label size in the dialog box that appears.

If you've selected the Full Page of the Same Label option, choosing New Document creates a new document consisting entirely of a sheet of labels. You can name and save this document and reuse it later.

LANGUAGE

1. Select the text that's in a different language.
2. Choose Tools, Language.
3. Choose a language under Mark Selected Text As.
4. Click on OK or press ENTER.

Marks the selected text as being in the specified language. This tells Word to hunt for the appropriate dictionary when it spell checks or otherwise proofs that particular text. Note that you can use as many languages as you like within a single document, provided that the needed dictionary files are installed. (Consult Microsoft Corporation for details on purchasing and installing dictionaries.) To prevent a certain area of your document from being proofed, select it and then choose [no proofing] under Mark Selected Text As.

To change which language is used by default during spell checks and other proofing operations, highlight the desired language in the Language dialog box and then choose the Default button. This changes the default language for the current template. Besides using the dictionaries listed by the Language command, you can create your own custom dictionaries, as described under SPELL CHECKING.

LINE BREAKS

1. Place the insertion point where you want to end one line and begin another.
2. Press SHIFT+ENTER.

Inserts a line break character, which starts a new line without creating a new paragraph. This lets you enter multiple lines but format them as a single paragraph. Line break characters (leftward-pointing arrows) show up if you press the Show/Hide button on the Standard toolbar.

Don't confuse line breaks with paragraph marks, which you insert simply by pressing ENTER. Pressing ENTER creates a new paragraph, which you can single out for many types of paragraph formatting—indents and line spacing, for example.

Since Word for Windows word wraps your text (proceeding to the next line when you have filled a line with text) you don't generally need to press ENTER or SHIFT+ENTER to start a new line of text. Only do so when you want to create a shorter line or insert a blank line. (See "Entering Text" under "General Procedures.")

LINE NUMBERS

1. Place the insertion point in the section whose lines you want to number.
2. Choose File, Page Setup.
3. If necessary, click on the Layout tab.
4. Choose Line Numbers and select the Add Line Numbering check box.
5. Click on OK or press ENTER, and then click on OK or press ENTER to leave the Page Setup dialog box.

Numbers the lines in the designated section, situating the line numbers in the margins or between columns. If the document is not divided into sections, this numbers the entire document. See SECTIONS. Line numbers only show up in Page Layout view or Print Preview. (If you don't see the numbers, change the zoom setting to 75% or less.) To remove line numbers, follow the preceding steps but deselect the Add Line Numbering check box.

In the Line Numbers dialog box, you can specify a different number in the Start At box to have numbering begin at a value other than 1. Under From Text, you can indicate the distance between text and line numbers. Under Count By, you can specify a numbering increment other than 1; choose 2 to number every other line, for instance. Finally, under Numbering you can choose whether to have the numbering restart on each page (the default), restart in each section, or be continuous throughout the document.

To remove line numbering for one or more specified paragraphs, place the insertion point within a single paragraph or select several paragraphs, choose Format, Paragraph, choose the Text Flow tab if necessary, select

Suppress Line Numbers, and then click on OK or press
ENTER. This does not just conceal line numbers from view,
but actually omits the paragraphs in question from the
line numbering sequence.

LINKING

You can establish *links* between one Word document and
another, and between Word documents and documents
created in other applications. Links let you use
information from other sources in your Word documents.
You can also *embed* material from other sources into your
Word documents. This places an actual copy of the data
in your Word file, rather than just a field code indicating a
link. (See EMBEDDING.)

When you create a link, you're inserting a *field code* in a
Word document that tells Word to retrieve information
from another document (see FIELDS). The Word
document containing the field code is often called the
destination file, while the document supplying the data is
called the *source file.* Once you forge a link between files,
changes in the source file are automatically reflected in
the destination file, ensuring that the linked data in your
Word file is always up to date.

Breaking Links

1. Choose Edit, Links.
2. Choose the link(s) that you want to break.
3. Click on the Break Link button and then choose Yes.

Keyboard Shortcut:

CTRL+SHIFT+F9   Breaks the selected link(s)

Breaks the designated link or links, severing the
connection between the source and destination files. The
information in the destination document is not removed,
but since it is no longer connected to the source
document it cannot reflect any new changes. To
temporarily prevent changes in the source file from being
reflected in the destination file, lock the link instead (see
"Locking Links").

Creating Links

To link a Word document with another Word document or
with a document from another application:

1. Make sure Word and the other application are both
   running and switch to the other (source) application.

2. Open the file with which you want to establish a link.

3. Use the Edit, Copy command to place the information to
   be linked on the Clipboard. You can copy the entire file
   or only a portion of it.

4. Switch to Word and open the document in which you
   want to establish a link, placing the insertion point
   where you want the linked information to go. (If you're
   not sure how to switch between applications, consult a
   Windows text or your Windows documentation.)

5. Choose Edit, Paste Special.

6. Select Paste Link and choose the desired option under
   As. (See the descriptions under Result or your Word
   documentation for details.)

7. Click on OK or press ENTER.

You can also create a link by opening another application
while within Word for Windows:

1. Open the Word document in which you want to
   establish a link.

2. Choose Insert, Object.

3. If necessary, choose the Create from File tab.

4. Under File Name, specify which file you want to
   establish a link with. (If necessary, make selections
   under Directories and Drives to track down the file.

5. Make sure the Link to File check box is selected and
   choose Display as Icon if you want to see the linked
   object as an icon.

6. Click on OK or press ENTER.

Establishes a link between two Word files or between a
Word file and a file from another application. Once files
are linked, changes in the source file are usually reflected
in the destination file automatically. (You can also
establish manual links, which are updated only at your
request; see "Updating Links.") If you link files using the
Insert, Object command, you can only insert entire files;
if you use Edit, Paste Special, in contrast, you can choose
which portion of the file to link.

Locking Links

1. Open the Word document containing the link(s) to be locked.
2. Choose Edit, Links.
3. Choose the link(s) that you wish to lock.
4. Select the Locked check box.
5. Click on OK or press ENTER.

Keyboard Shortcuts:

CTRL+F11   Locks the selected link(s)

CTRL+SHIFT+F11   Unlocks the selected link(s)

Locks the selected links, temporarily preventing them from being updated when there are changes in the source file. You can also unlock links to reactivate the connection between the source and destination files by following the preceding steps but deselecting the Locked check box.

Updating Links

To determine whether links are updated automatically or manually:

1. Choose Edit, Links.
2. Choose the desired link(s).
3. Choose Automatic or Manual.
4. Click on OK or press ENTER.

To update manual links:

1. Choose Edit, Links.
2. Choose the link(s) that you want to update.
3. Choose Update Now and then choose Close.

To have links updated automatically whenever you print

1. Choose Tools, Options.
2. Select the Print tab, if it's not already selected.
3. Under Printing Options, select Update Links.
4. Click on OK or press ENTER.

Keyboard Shortcut:

F9   Updates the selected link(s)

Determines what type of links you have in your document and when they are updated with current information from the source document. Automatic links are updated automatically when you open the Word document that contains them. They are also updated if you update the source file while the destination file is open within Word for Windows. Manual links, by contrast, are updated only when you specifically request it.

MACROS

Macros are shortcuts for command sequences. Once you've created a macro, you can repeat a very complex series of commands in a few easy steps. You can create macros that run when you press a certain combination of keys and can even assign macros to menu options and toolbar buttons.

You can also rename, copy, and delete macros in the Organizer (see ORGANIZER), and can edit macros. (Editing macros requires a knowledge of WordBasic and is beyond the scope of this book. If you're interested, consult the on-line help system or your Microsoft Word documentation.)

Deleting Macros

1. Choose Tools, Macro.
2. Choose the desired macro(s) under Macro Name.
3. Choose the Delete button and respond Yes to the prompt.

Deletes the selected macros. Also see ORGANIZER.

Recording Macros

1. Choose Tools, Macro.
2. Choose Record.
3. Type a macro name of up to 36 characters under Record Macro Name. (Don't use commas, periods, or spaces.)
4. If you like, type a macro description of up to 255 characters under Description.
5. Choose the OK button, noting that the Macro Record toolbar appears on screen and the mouse pointer has a recorder icon attached to it.

6. Perform the actions that you want recorded as a macro.

7. Choose Tools, Macro and then click on Stop Recording; choose Close if you want to close the Macro dialog box.

Mouse Shortcuts:

Double-click REC indicator in status bar	Opens Record Macro dialog box; or stops macro recording
	Stops macro recording
	Pauses macro recording; or resumes it if it's paused

Creates a macro that you can "play back" (run) later, performing the recorded series of commands with very little effort. When recording macros, you must use keyboard techniques to move the insertion point and to select text. When selecting from menus and dialog boxes, you are free to use the mouse.

Choosing Toolbars, Menus, or Keyboard in the Record Macro dialog box brings up the Customize dialog box with the appropriate tab selected. This lets you assign frequently used macros to shortcut keys, toolbar buttons, or menu options—making it that much easier to play them back. If you do so, it's a good idea to enter a description in the Record Macro dialog box, since this text will show up at the bottom of the screen when you highlight the menu option or place the mouse pointer over the toolbar button. Note that you create the custom toolbar button, shortcut key, or menu item first, and then record the macro as described above. (See CUSTOMIZE.)

If the current document is associated with a template other than the Normal template, you can select either that template or the Normal template under Make Macro Available To in the Record Macro dialog box to determine where the macro is stored. Macros are stored in the Normal template by default, where they are available in all documents. (See TEMPLATES.)

Running Macros

1. If applicable, move the insertion point to the desired spot or select the text to be affected.

2. Choose Tools, Macro.

3. If necessary, decide which type of macro to choose from under the Macros Available In box.

4. Under Macro Name, choose the macro you want to run.

5. Click on Run or press ENTER.

Runs the selected macro, "playing back" the entire sequence of commands stored within it. (The preceding section explains how to create macros.) If you use a particular macro frequently, it's best to assign it to a keyboard shortcut, menu, or toolbar button so that you don't have to go through the Macro dialog box each time you want to execute that series of commands.

By default, the Macros Available In box instructs Word to list the macros in all currently available templates. You can also display just the macros in the Normal template. In addition, you can choose to see an alphabetical list of every Word command; to execute any command from here, highlight it and choose Run or press ENTER.

MAIL MERGE

Word for Windows' Mail Merge feature enables you to create form letters, envelopes, mailing labels, and more. To do so, you merge a *main document* (constant data such as the text of a form letter) with a *data source* (varying data such as names and addresses). Special codes called *merge fields* in the main document direct Word to collect information from the data source and weave it into the main document—placing a name directly after the salutation "Dear," for example—to create a series of personalized letters, labels, or envelopes.

There are three basic steps involved in a mail merge: You must designate an existing main document and edit it if necessary, or create a new main document; you must choose an existing data source, or create a new one; and, finally, you must perform the merge operation. Especially when you're setting up a mail merge for the first time (putting together a main document and constructing a data source), Mail Merge can take some time to master. If necessary, see your Word for Windows documentation or the on-line help system for additional details.

Choosing the Main Document

1. Open an existing document or create a new document to be used as the main document. Add as much or as little text as you like. Since you'll need to return to this document later to insert merge fields, you can make changes and additions at that point.

2. Choose Tools, Mail Merge.

3. Click on the Create button and choose Form Letters.

4. Choose Active Window to make active document into the main document.

Designates which document will be used as the main document. Next, you have to designate or create the data source. Once you've done so, you can go back and refine the main document, adding merge fields and formatting, adding, and editing text as desired.

If you open a main document that has already been set up for a mail merge, you don't need to perform the preceding steps. You can simply define a new data source and go ahead with the merge operation, as described in a moment. (And if you want to reuse the data source used in the last merge operation, you can simply perform the merge.)

Defining the Data Source

To create a new data source:

1. If necessary, choose a main document, as described in "Choosing the Main Document."

2. From within the Mail Merge Helper dialog box, choose Get Data under Data Source.

3. Select Create Data Source.

4. In the Field Names in Header Row list box, choose which types of information to include in the data source. Delete field names by highlighting them and selecting Remove Field Name; add field names by typing them under Field Name and selecting Add Field Name; and move field names by highlighting them and pressing the arrows above and below the word "Move."

5. When the Field Names in Header Row list box contains the categories of information you want to include in your data source, choose OK.

6. In the Save Data Source dialog box, enter a name for the new data source document under File Name and click on OK or press ENTER.

7. Choose the Edit Data Source button.

8. In the Data Form dialog box, type the requisite data in each text box. When you're done entering one record (set of data), choose Add New or press ENTER to start creating a new record. Note that you can press TAB and SHIFT+TAB to move forward and backward through the fields, in case you need to make changes.

9. Repeat the preceding step as many times as needed to enter all the information you need into your data source.

10. Choose OK to close the Data Form dialog box.

Creates a new data source consisting of the records you've just entered.

You can also open an existing data source, as described here:

1. If necessary, choose a main document, as described above.

2. From within the Mail Merge Helper dialog box (choose Tools, Mail Merge, if necessary), choose Get Data under Data Source.

3. Choose Open Data Source.

4. Under File Name, select the desired data source and then click on OK or press ENTER. (If necessary, select a new drive and/or directory, make a different selection in the List Files of Type drop-down list box, or use Find File to find the data source you seek.)

5. If your main document does not already contain merge fields, choose Edit Main Document. Now you can finish the main document, as described in the next section.

Determines which data source Word will use when performing a mail merge. After creating a data source or opening an existing data source, you may need to complete the main document by adding merge fields and making any other final additions or alterations. (If you're using an existing main document that already contains the desired merge fields, you can skip straight to performing the merge operation.)

Finishing the Main Document

1. Make sure your main document is open and, if necessary, type and format any text that you want repeated (such as the main body of a form letter).

2. Position the insertion point where you want to place the information that will vary (such as the name and address), and select the Insert Merge Field button on the Mail Merge toolbar.

3. Choose the desired merge field from list.

4. Repeat steps 2 and 3 as needed to insert all the desired merge fields into the main document. (Don't forget to include spaces and commas where needed—between city and state codes, as an example.)

5. Choose File, Save to save the main document.

Completes the main document. Once you've created or opened a data source and completed the main document by adding merge fields as well as any other finishing touches, you're ready to perform a merge operation.

If you are working with an existing main document that already contains merge fields, you needn't perform the preceding steps, although you can use this procedure to make alterations to the document's text or merge fields.

Performing the Merge Operation

1. Open the main document if it's not already opened.

2. Choose Tools, Mail Merge.

3. Confirm that the desired data source is listed under Data Source in the Mail Merge Helper dialog box. (If not, review the section "Defining the Data Source.")

4. Click on the Merge button in the Mail Merge Helper dialog box.

5. In the Merge dialog box, choose whether to merge to a new document or the printer, which records to merge, and whether to print blank lines if data fields are empty. Then click on Merge or press ENTER.

6. If you merged to the printer, make any needed selections from the Print dialog box and then click on OK or press ENTER.

7. When the merge is completed, click on Cancel to close the Mail Merge Helper dialog box.

Mouse Shortcuts:

 Lets you preview merged documents before performing merge

 Lets you merge to a new document

 Lets you merge to the printer

 Opens the Merge dialog box

 Opens the associated data source for editing

Merges the main document and data source, replacing merge fields with the appropriate data from the data source and generating as many merged documents as there are records in the data source. You can either merge to a new file, or you can merge directly to the printer to have your personalized documents printed right away.

Note that Word remembers which data source file was used with which main document. This enables you to repeat a merge operation simply by opening the main document, choosing Tools, Mail Merge, and going ahead with the merge as described above. You also have the option of refining or altering the main document or data source by choosing Edit under either Main Document or Data Source in the Mail Merge Helper dialog box; you can also edit the main document directly on the screen. In other words, repeating a mail merge operation can be a great deal easier than setting one up for the first time.

Producing Labels and Envelopes with Mail Merge

To create envelopes:

1. Open a new document and choose Tools, Mail Merge.
2. Choose Create under Main Document and select Envelopes.
3. Choose Active Window.
4. Choose Get Data, and then either open an existing data source or create a new data source.
5. If you choose an existing data source, choose Set Up Main Document to get into the Envelope Options dialog box. If you choose to create a new data source, follow

the instructions under "Defining the Data Source" above. After closing the Data Form dialog box, choose Tools, Mail Merge and choose Setup in the Mail Merge Helper dialog box to get into the Envelope Options dialog box.

6. On the Envelope Options tab, choose an envelope size and change the font and position of the delivery address and return address, if necessary.

7. Choose the Printing Options tab, make any necessary changes, and then click on OK or press ENTER.

8. Choose Insert Merge Field and insert the desired merge fields in the Sample Envelope Address text box, placing each field where you want it to appear in the merged envelopes. Choose OK when you're done.

9. If necessary, prepare your printer to print envelopes and click on Merge under Merge the Data with the Document.

10. In the Merge dialog box, choose whether to merge to a new document or the printer, which records to merge, and whether to print blank lines if data fields are empty. Then click on Merge.

11. If you merged to the printer, make any needed selections from the Print dialog box and then click on OK or press ENTER.

12. When the merge is completed, click on Cancel to close the Mail Merge Helper dialog box.

13. When you're done producing envelopes, save your document (File, Save As) so you can use it to produce envelopes in the future.

To create labels:

1. Open a new document and choose Tools, Mail Merge.

2. Choose Create under Main Document and select Mailing Labels.

3. Choose Active Window.

4. Choose Get Data, and then either open an existing data source or create a new data source.

5. If you choose an existing data source, choose Set Up Main Document to get into the Label Options dialog box. If you choose to create a new data source, follow the instructions under "Defining the Data Source" above. After closing the Data Form dialog box, choose Tools, Mail Merge and choose Setup in the Mail Merge Helper dialog box to get into the Label Options dialog box.

6. In the Label Options dialog box, select a printer type if necessary, and choose a label type under Product Number. Then click on OK or press ENTER.

7. Choose Insert Merge Field and insert the desired merge fields in the Sample Label text box, placing each field where you want it to appear in the merged labels. Choose OK when you're done.

8. Prepare the printer to print labels and click on Merge under Merge the Data with the Document.

9. In the Merge dialog box, choose whether to merge to a new document or the printer, which records to merge, and whether to print blank lines if data fields are empty. Then click on Merge.

10. If you merged to the printer, make any needed selections from the Print dialog box and then click on OK or press ENTER.

11. When the merge is completed, click on Cancel to close the Mail Merge Helper dialog box.

12. When you're done producing labels, save your document (File, Save As) so you can use it to produce labels in the future.

Enables you to create envelopes or labels using the records in the designated data source. If you're doing a mass mailing, you're likely to need such labels or envelopes to complete the task.

As when creating merged documents such as form letters, once you've set up the main document, it is much easier to generate labels or envelopes in the future. Simply open the main document you want to use to create either envelopes or labels, choose Tools, Mail Merge, and choose the Merge button to proceed with the merge operation. From within the Mail Merge Helper dialog box, you can also choose a new data source, edit the data source, or edit the main document if you like.

MARGINS

1. Place the insertion point in the desired section, or select the text to be affected.

2. Choose File, Page Setup.

3. If necessary, click on the Margins tab.

4. Specify values under Top, Bottom, Left, and Right to change the margins.

5. Under <u>A</u>pply To, choose the portion of the document whose margins you want to change, if necessary.

6. Click on OK or press ENTER.

Changes the margins for the document as a whole, the current section, the selected text, or from the insertion point to the end of the document. (If you select the text to be affected, Word automatically inserts section breaks before and after it.) Keep in mind that margins demarcate where body text ends; headers, footers, page numbers, and other such elements are generally found in the margins.

When setting margins, you can choose the M<u>i</u>rror Margins check box if you're printing on both sides of the page. This way Word knows to treat odd and even pages differently, since the inside and outside margins differ on odd and even pages. You can also specify a value under G<u>u</u>tter if you wish to create larger inside margins to allow for bindings. Finally, once you've chosen the desired settings, you can make these the default settings for the current template by choosing the <u>D</u>efault button.

If you prefer to use the mouse, you can adjust the margins using your mouse and the rulers if you're in Page Layout view or Print Preview:

1. Place the insertion point in the section to be altered, or select the text you want to change.

2. Make sure the rulers are displayed. (If necessary, choose <u>V</u>iew, <u>R</u>uler to display them.)

3. Place the mouse pointer over the margin boundaries (where the grayed area of the ruler meets the white area); the pointer changes into a double-headed arrow. Then drag to move the margin, releasing the mouse button to deposit the margin in its new spot.

Enables you to change both the horizontal and vertical margins by eye. Hold down the ALT key while dragging to see measurements on the ruler.

MASTER DOCUMENTS

You can use *master documents* in order to more easily work with very long documents. You do this by dividing your document into a series of *subdocuments*, which are saved as individual files but which you can also work with as a group by using the master document.

You can work with master documents in Normal view or in Master Document view (a variation on Outline view). When you switch to Master Document view, the Master Document toolbar appears to the right of the Outlining toolbar. If necessary, familiarize yourself with Word's outlining feature before delving into master documents (see OUTLINING).

Creating Master Documents and Subdocuments

1. Open a new document.

2. Choose View, Master Document.

3. Type an outline, if necessary using the Outlining toolbar to assign heading levels. Make sure that the text that will mark the beginning of each subdocument has the same heading level. (For instance, if you want each chapter title to indicate where a new subdocument begins, assign the same heading level to all chapter titles.)

4. Select the headings (and any subtext) that you want to divide into subdocuments. The first heading you select tells Word where to partition the master document into subdocuments. If your selection begins with a level 2 head (the Heading 2 style), Word will create a new subdocument at each level 2 head within the selection.

5. Click on the Create Subdocument button on the Master Document toolbar. Word divides the master document into subdocuments, enclosing each one within a box and displaying a subdocument icon to its left.

6. Choose File, Save As, enter a name for the master document, and click on OK or press ENTER. Word automatically names and saves all associated subdocuments.

Mouse Shortcuts:

   Creates subdocuments from selected text

   Inserts a document as a subdocument

Creates a master document containing subdocuments that you can work on separately. You can also change existing documents into master documents: Just open the desired document, switch to Master Document view, and alter the document's headings as needed using the Outlining toolbar. (You must use Word's built-in heading styles; see STYLES.) Then, follow the steps described above.

You can add subdocuments to master documents that you have already created. Make sure the desired master document is open, put the insertion point where you want to place the new subdocument, click on the Insert Subdocument button on the Master Document toolbar, choose the desired file from the Insert Subdocument dialog box, and then click on OK or press ENTER.

Using Master Documents

Work on the master document when you want to operate on any and all subdocuments and have all changes recorded in the master document. Also open the master document when you want to perform tasks, such as indexing, that affect the document as a whole.

You can work on your master document either in Normal view or in Master Document view. Switch to Master Document view to get an overview of the larger document. Although you can still see your entire document in this view, you have more flexibility to manipulate it. You can easily create and open subdocuments, promote and demote headings, collapse and expand your outline, and perform many of the other tasks associated with outlining (see OUTLINING). Note that you can also apply formatting (such as pagination) that you want to affect the entire master document—just make sure that you're in the master document, not within a subdocument. (To apply formatting to an individual subdocument, just position yourself within that subdocument before you proceed.)

When you instead want to treat all subdocuments in your master document as one very long document, switch to Normal view. For example, to print the entire master document as straight text, first switch to Normal view.

Using Subdocuments

Opening subdocuments:

1. Open the subdocument's master document and make sure you're in Master Document view.

2. Double-click on the subdocument icon. (You can also use the File, Open command, but don't do this if you plan to rename or move the document.)

3. Make the desired additions or corrections to the subdocument.

4. When you're done, save the subdocument under the same name. This saves the changes both to the subdocument and to the master document it's associated with.

Moving subdocuments to a different location in the master document:

1. Open the master document and switch to Master Document view.

2. Click on the subdocument icon, use it to drag the subdocument to the desired spot, and release the mouse button.

Combining subdocuments:

1. Open the master document and switch to Master Document view.

2. Move the subdocuments to be merged so that they're adjacent.

3. Click on the icon of one of the subdocuments to be merged.

4. Hold down the SHIFT key and click on the icons of other subdocuments you want to combine.

5. Click on the Merge Subdocument button on the Master Document toolbar.

Dividing subdocuments:

1. Open the master document and switch to Master Document view.

2. Place the insertion point where you want the split to occur.

3. Click on the Split Subdocument button on the Master Document toolbar.

4. Choose File, Save to save the newly created subdocument.

Deleting subdocuments from the master document:

1. Open the master document and make sure you're in Master Document view.

2. Click on the icon of the subdocument to be deleted.

3. Press DEL or BACKSPACE.

Locking and unlocking subdocuments:

1. Open the master document and make sure you're in Master Document view.

2. Place the insertion point within the subdocument you wish to lock or unlock.

3. Click on the Lock Document button on the Master Document toolbar.

Lets you lock or unlock documents so you can make changes to them. Word subdocuments are locked to you if they've been created by someone else. Subdocuments are also locked if you open them individually and then open the master document; in this case you have to close the open subdocument before you can unlock it from within the master document.

Mouse Shortcuts:

 Merges selected subdocument back in with master document

 Merges the selected subdocuments

 Splits the current subdocument at the insertion point

 Locks or unlocks the current subdocument

MOVING TEXT AND GRAPHICS

See CUT AND PASTE, DRAG AND DROP, and SPIKE.

MULTILEVEL LISTS

1. Choose Format, Bullets and Numbering.

2. If necessary, choose the Multilevel tab.

3. Choose the desired format, or click on Modify to create a customized format.

4. Click on OK or press ENTER.

5. Type your list. To create lower level headings, press ALT+SHIFT+RIGHT ARROW or click on the Increase Indent button on the Formatting toolbar. To create higher level headings, press ALT+SHIFT+LEFT ARROW or click on the

Decrease Indent button. (This is often referred to as "promoting" and "demoting" headings.)

Mouse Shortcuts:

 Increases indent and moves to next lowest level in multilevel list

 Decreases indent and moves to next highest level in multilevel list

Enables you to create a list with up to nine heading levels. You can also select existing text and apply a multilevel list format to it; Word will guess at the appropriate heading level, and you can promote or demote headings as needed. You can remove the list formatting by selecting the list and then choosing the Remove button on the Multilevel tab in the Bullets and Numbering dialog box.

The multilevel list feature is handy for certain legal documents and for outlines. However, if you want to expand your outline into a full-fledged document, you should probably use Word's outlining feature instead. This way you can collapse your outline to get an overview, and can more easily reorganize and manipulate it in a variety of ways. (See OUTLINING.)

NEW FILE

1. Choose File, New.
2. Under Template, choose the template or wizard upon which to base the new document.
3. Ensure that Document (not Template) is selected.
4. Click on OK or press ENTER.

Keyboard Shortcut:
CTRL+N   Opens a new document using the Normal template

Mouse Shortcut:
 Opens a new document using the Normal template

Creates a new document, using the designated template or wizard. The new document is supplied with a temporary name, such as Document1 or Document2, that you can change when you save. Note that templates are basic document designs, which may just include minimal formatting specifications, and may also include text and quite specific document layout information. Wizards, in contrast, guide you through the process of creating a particular type of document. See also OPENING FILES, SUMMARY INFO, TEMPLATES, WIZARDS.

NUMBERED LISTS

1. Select the paragraphs you want to transform into a numbered list.
2. Choose Format, Bullets and Numbering.
3. If necessary, select the Numbered tab.
4. Choose the desired numbering style, or click on Modify to create a customized format.
5. Click on OK or press ENTER.

Mouse Shortcut:

 Inserts numbers in front of selected paragraphs, or removes numbers if they're already there

Transforms the selected paragraphs into a numbered list that has the designated numbering style. Retain the hanging indent to have the number sit to the left of all text, instead of having text wrap underneath it.

See BULLETS, MULTILEVEL LISTS, NUMBERING HEADINGS, and OUTLINING for other ways to organize your thoughts.

If you need to remove the numbering, select the list and then choose the Remove button on the Numbered tab, or click again on the Numbering button on the Formatting toolbar. To remove numbering from just a portion of the list, select the text in question, click the right mouse button to bring up the shortcut menu, and choose either Skip Numbering or Stop Numbering. Skip Numbering removes numbering from the selected items and resumes numbering where it left off for any subsequent items. Stop Numbering, in contrast, removes numbering from the selected items and resumes numbering at 1 for any subsequent items.

NUMBERING HEADINGS

1. Choose Format, Heading Numbering.
2. Select the desired number format, or click on Modify to create a customized format.
3. Click on OK or press ENTER.

Applies numbered headings to all heads in your document that have been formatted with Word's built-in heading styles; see STYLES. (In contrast, the multilevel list feature applies numbering to all text, rather than just to headings.) This operation affects all sections in your document. If you decide to remove heading numbering from a particular section, place the insertion point within it, issue the Format, Heading Numbering command, and choose the Remove button. See also BULLETS, MULTILEVEL LISTS, NUMBERED LISTS, and OUTLINING.

You can easily modify the heading numbering scheme: In the Heading Numbering dialog box, click on the Modify button. Pick the heading level to be affected by scrolling to choose a Level. Now you can change the font and the style of the bullet or number character, specify any text that you want to appear before or after the various numbering characters, designate a new starting number, and determine the position of the bullet or number character. Make changes for as many levels (up to 9) as you want. In addition, note that you can choose to have numbering start over in each new section.

OBJECTS

See EMBEDDING.

OPENING FILES

1. Choose File, Open.
2. Choose a file under File Name. (If necessary, change drives and/or directories, or choose a new selection under List Files of Type, to find the desired file.)
3. Click on OK or press ENTER.

Keyboard Shortcut:

CTRL+O   Displays the Open dialog box

Mouse Shortcut:

                Displays the Open dialog box

Opens the designated file. You can open more than one
file at a time by dragging over several files, or by
highlighting the first file, holding down the CTRL key, and
clicking on additional files. Then click on OK or press
ENTER. You can open as many files as your computer's
memory permits. Typically, only one open document
shows up on the screen; see WINDOWS for information
on how to work with and display several documents at
once. (See also "Opening and Closing Files" under
"General Procedures" for more information on opening
files.)

Although you generally needn't close one file to open
another, it's good practice to close files that you no longer
plan to work with (see CLOSING FILES). To create a new
file rather than opening an existing one, use the New
command on the File menu (see NEW FILE).

Under Directories in the Open dialog box, you can
double-click on a directory name to display all of its
subdirectories and list all the files it contains under File
Name. If you double-click on a directory that has no
subdirectories, Word simply displays all files from that
directory, if there are any. Under Drives, you can select a
different drive whose files you want to view. You can also
make selections from the List Files of Type drop-down
list box to determine which types of files show up in the
File Name list box. You can also enter file specifications
directly into the File Name text box.

If you can't remember where you stored a particular file,
you can click on the Find File button and hunt for the file
using the Find File feature (see FINDING FILES). If you
want a different directory's files displayed by default in
the Open dialog box, see DIRECTORIES.

You can open a file as read-only by checking the Read
Only check box. You can view read-only files, but you
cannot change them and then save them under the same
name. (You can, however, make changes and then save
the file with a new name.) See PASSWORDS and
PROTECTING DOCUMENTS for details on additional
ways of guarding your documents against changes.

You can easily reopen the files you've opened most recently just by selecting them from the bottom of the File menu. If you like, you can even change how many files are displayed at the bottom of the File menu; see "General" under OPTIONS for details.

Finally, Word includes a number of *converters* that recognize other file formats and convert them into a format that Word can contend with. If the proper converter is installed, you can use files created in other applications—including WordPerfect, Excel, Lotus 1-2-3, and others—simply by opening them, as described earlier in this section.

OPTIONS

The Options dialog box is your main means of customizing Word to suit your wants and your tastes. (Also see CUSTOMIZE for details about how to tailor Word's menus, toolbars, and keyboard shortcuts to your liking.) It is here that you establish how Word carries out various operations, determine much of what you see on the screen, and choose where files are stored. To work in the Options dialog box, choose Tools, Options, and select the desired tab. The available options are described next.

AutoFormat

The AutoFormat tab in the Options dialog box determines how documents are formatted when you use the AutoFormat command. Select the Previously Applied Styles check box if you do not want AutoFormat operations to do away with styles you have applied to the document (see STYLES). Under Apply Styles To, you can decide which items Word will apply styles to automatically. Under Adjust, you can have Word standardize specified spacing elements. For example, if you select Tabs and Spaces, Word substitutes tabs for spaces where appropriate. Under Replace, you can determine which characters to replace during an AutoFormat operation, and with what. For instance, if you select Straight Quotes with Smart Quotes, Word changes all quotation marks to curly quotes.

Compatibility

The Compatibility tab in the Options dialog box lets you decide how Word will show documents created either in earlier versions of Word or in other word processors. Select Font Substitution if the fonts used in the original document are not available in the current context and you need to substitute similar fonts. Under Recommended Options For, choose a word processing program to see Word's recommended options for that particular program The various selections that you make under Options will affect how documents are displayed in Word (but will not actually change the documents). Choose the Default button to save the selected options as the default for the current template.

Edit

The Edit tab in the Options dialog box lets you change certain of Word's editing settings.

- Select Typing Replaces Selection to be able to select text and then have it replaced with what you type.

- Select Drag-and-Drop Text Editing to be able to move or copy selected text by dragging (see DRAG AND DROP).

- Select Automatic Word Selection to have Word automatically highlight entire words only when you drag to select multiple words; deselect this option to be able to select partial words with your mouse.

- Select Use the INS Key for Paste if you want to use the INS key to insert material from the Clipboard rather than to switch between insert and overtype modes.

- Select Overtype Mode to put Word in overtype mode by default (text will be replaced instead of pushed aside as you add new text); you'll still be able to switch between insert and overtype modes (see INSERT MODE and OVERTYPE MODE).

- Select Use Smart Cut and Paste to have Word add or delete spaces as needed when you move text.

- Select Allow Accented Uppercase to have Word permit you to use uppercase accented letters in text that is marked as French (see LANGUAGE).

- Select options under Picture Editor to choose which application Word uses as the picture editor (the application that Word opens when you double-click on an imported graphic in preparation for editing it).

File Locations

The File Locations Tab in the Options dialog box lets you determine where certain file and template types are stored by default. See DIRECTORIES.

General

The General tab in the Options dialog box lets you change a variety of general settings in Word for Windows.

- Select Background Repagination to have repagination occur automatically.

- If you're a former WordPerfect user, select Help for Word-Perfect Users so you can press WordPerfect keystrokes and see their Word equivalents.

- Select Navigation Keys for WordPerfect Users to change the PGUP, PGDN, HOME, END, and ESC keys to their Word-Perfect functions.

- Select Blue Background, White Text to change the Word for Windows display as described.

- Select Beep On Error Actions to get auditory reprimands when you make mistakes.

- Select 3D Dialog and Display Effects to turn on certain color and three-dimensional effects in dialog boxes.

- Select Update Automatic Links at Open to have Word update any automatic links in files that you open.

- Select Mail As Attachment to have Word attach documents to mail messages, if an e-mail program is installed.

- Select Recently Used File List to be able to decide how many names of recently used files show up near the bottom of the File menu.

- Select Measurement Units to be able to choose which units of measurement Word uses by default in rulers and dialog box settings. (See RULER.)

Grammar

The Grammar tab in the Options dialog box lets you identify which grammar rules will be used during grammar checks. Under Use Grammar and Style Rules, choose among various sets of rules that will be used during grammar checks. You can even create custom sets of rules; just click on the Customize Settings button and make selections from the Customize Grammar Settings dialog box that appears. The Check Spelling check box lets you determine whether Word checks spelling while carrying out grammar checks. The Show Readability Statistics check box lets you decide whether to see a list of "readability statistics"—including word count and character count—after grammar checks. Also see GRAMMAR CHECKING.

Print

The Print tab in the Options dialog box determines what settings Word uses when it prints your documents, as well as what elements it includes in the printout. Also see PRINTING.

- Select Draft Output to print quickly and with minimal formatting.
- Select Reverse Print Order to print the last page first and the first page last.
- Select Update Fields to have Word update fields automatically when printing.
- Choose Update Links to have Word update any links before printing.
- Select Background Printing to be able to keep working in Word while printing occurs (this may slow printing).
- Select Summary Info to print the document's summary information.
- Select Field Codes to print field codes rather than their results.
- Select Annotations to print annotations on a separate page.
- Select Hidden Text to print any hidden text in your document.
- Select Drawing Objects to print drawing objects such as charts and graphics.
- Select Print Data Only for Forms to print only input typed into form fields; select this option if you're printing onto preprinted forms.
- Select Default Tray to choose printer trays.

Revisions

The Revisions tab in the Options dialog box lets you choose and customize revision marks, determining how added text, deleted text, and revised lines are marked and colored. (Choose By Author to have Word automatically assign different colors to comments by different reviewers.) Consult the Preview boxes for samples of how the revised text might appear. Also see REVISIONS.

Save

The Save tab in the Options dialog box determines how and when Word conducts save operations. See also SAVE, SAVE ALL, SAVE AS.

- Select Always Create Backup Copy to have Word create extra file copies with the .BAK extension when it saves files.

- Select Allow Fast Saves to speed up save operations by having Word only save changes rather than the entire document.

- Select Prompt for Summary Info to have Word bring up the Summary Info dialog box whenever you save.

- Select Prompt to Save Normal.dot to have Word ask you if you wish to retain changes in NORMAL.DOT, Word's default template.

- Select Save Native Picture Formats Only to have Word only save Windows versions of graphics that you import.

- Select Embed TrueType Fonts to tell Word to save True-Type fonts with the document so those exact fonts will be used whenever the document is viewed.

- Select Save Data Only for Forms to save a form's data but not the form itself.

- Select Automatically Save Every and specify a value under Minutes to tell Word to automatic save your document at a set interval.

- Type a password under Protection Password or Write Reservation Password to limit access to the active document. (You must save the document for the password to go into effect.) For details, see PASSWORDS and PRO-TECTING DOCUMENTS.

- Select <u>R</u>ead-Only Recommended to have Word recommend that the current file be opened as read-only the next time anyone opens the document.

Spelling

The Spelling tab in the Options dialog box lets you make choices about how Word carries out spell checks. See also SPELL CHECKING.

- Select A<u>l</u>ways Suggest to have Word always suggest alternate spellings when it comes up with them.

- Select From <u>M</u>ain Dictionary Only to have Word display alternate spellings from the main dictionary but not from any open custom dictionaries.

- Select Words in <u>U</u>PPERCASE to tell Word not to spell check uppercase words.

- Select Words with Num<u>b</u>ers to instruct Word not to check the spelling of words that include numbers.

- Select Reset <u>I</u>gnore All to tell Word to no longer ignore words that you marked with Ignore All during a spell check operation.

- Under Custom <u>D</u>ictionaries, <u>N</u>ew enables you to create a custom dictionary; <u>E</u>dit lets you open and edit an existing custom dictionary; <u>A</u>dd permits you to add a dictionary from other source; and <u>R</u>emove lets you take a selected dictionary off the list of custom dictionaries.

- Select a language from the Language drop-down list box with a custom dictionary highlighted to have Word use that particular dictionary when checking text formatted in the designated language.

User Info

The User Info tab in the Options dialog box lets you enter the name, initials, and mailing address of the person who uses this particular copy of Word most often. Word uses this information in annotation marks and as the default return address, among other things.

View

The View tab in the Options dialog box enables you to determine which nonprinting characters show up on the editing screen, and also to remove or restore screen elements such as scroll bars and rulers. The available options on the View tab vary depending on what view you're in (see "The Different Views" under "General Procedures"). You can change a few display options (such as the display of the horizontal ruler and of various toolbars) through the <u>V</u>iew menu instead.

- Select <u>D</u>raft Font to have Word replace character formatting with underlining and boldfacing, and display empty boxes rather than graphics (Outline view and Normal view only).

- Select Dra<u>w</u>ings (Page Layout view only) to display drawings; deselect this option (and hide drawings) to speed up the display.

- Select <u>O</u>bject Anchors (Page Layout view only) to display the anchors that attach objects to paragraphs.

- Select <u>W</u>rap to Window (Outline view and Normal view only) to have Word rewrap the text to always fit within the left and right borders of the document window as you resize the window.

- Select Te<u>x</u>t Boundaries (Page Layout view only) to introduce dotted lines that show margins, columns, objects, and frames.

- Select <u>P</u>icture Placeholders to display empty boxes in the place of graphics; this speeds up your display.

- Select <u>F</u>ield Codes to have Word display field codes rather than field results (see FIELDS).

- Select Boo<u>k</u>marks to have Word display bookmarks and links, enclosed within gray brackets.

- Use the Fi<u>e</u>ld Shading drop-down list box to determine whether and when fields are shaded.

- Select Status <u>B</u>ar to display the status bar at the bottom of the screen; deselect this check box to hide the status bar.

- Select Hori<u>z</u>ontal Scroll Bar or <u>V</u>ertical Scroll Bar to display Word's scroll bars; deselect these check boxes to hide scroll bars.

- Specify a positive value under Style Area Width (Normal view and Outline view only) to display the *style area* to the left of your text; this area lists which styles are applied to each paragraph in your document. (See STYLES.) Close the style area by entering a value of 0.

- Select the Vertical Ruler check box (Page Layout and Print Preview only) to display the vertical ruler; deselect this check box to conceal the vertical ruler.

- Under Nonprinting Characters, select Tab Characters, Spaces, Paragraph Marks, Optional Hyphens, Hidden Text, and All to display those nonprinting characters on your screen. Select All (or use the Show/Hide button on the Standard toolbar) to show all nonprinting characters. Deselect these check boxes to remove the designated items from view.

ORGANIZER

You can use Word's Organizer to manage your macros, AutoText entries, toolbars, and styles—renaming them, deleting them, and copying them between templates. To do so, choose Templates from the File menu and then choose the Organizer button. Select the desired tab, and proceed from there. See also AUTOTEXT, MACROS, STYLES, and TOOLBARS.

You can delete and rename AutoText entries, macros, styles, and toolbars, as well as copy them between templates. To delete any one of these items, choose the desired dialog box tab, highlight the item's name, select the Delete button, and respond Yes to the confirmation prompt. Make sure you're deleting the item from the desired template; check the template name (it will have the .DOT extension) above the highlighted item. To rename an item, highlight its name, choose the Rename button, type a new name under New Name, and click on OK or press ENTER. If necessary, choose the desired template under Available In to find the correct item. If the template you want is not open, choose the Close File button to close the current template, and then choose Open File to open the desired template.

To copy an AutoText entry, macro, style, or toolbar from one template to another, first choose the templates you want to copy the items to and from by making selections under Available In. (If the current document is associated with the Normal template, only that template will be available. To open a new template, click on Close File, click on Open File, and then choose a template from the list that appears.) Next choose the item to be copied. When you choose <u>C</u>opy, the highlighted item will be copied to the designated template.

You can delete, rename, and copy custom toolbars, but cannot move, rename, or delete the toolbars provided with Word. (You can customize them, however, as described under CUSTOMIZE.)

OUTLINING

You use Word's outlining feature, not just to create outlines per se, but to build documents that you can "collapse" to varying degrees to get an overview, "expand" once again to see in greater detail, and more easily rethink and reorganize. To use Word's outlining feature, you switch to Outline view. (When creating outlines that you don't intend to develop into full-fledged documents, you may want to use the multilevel list feature; see MULTILEVEL LISTS.)

When you open a new document in Outline view, Word automatically applies its built-in heading styles to text that you type. It formats different heading levels in different sizes and styles, and indents subheadings—that is, it displays your document in outline form. You can easily instruct Word to create lower-level headings, higher-level headings, or regular body text. (You can apply Word's nine heading level styles in any view; it's just easier to do so in Outline view. For details, see STYLES.) Many of the operations that you perform in Outline view—including collapsing and expanding your outline—are predicated on these different heading levels.

Creating Outlines

1. Open a new document and make sure you're in Outline view. (Choose <u>V</u>iew, <u>O</u>utline or click on the Outline view button in the lower-left corner of the screen.)

2. Type text for a heading. (Word will automatically format it as a level 1 heading.)

3. To create more headings at the same level, just press ENTER and type in the heading text.

4. To create headings at a lower level, press ENTER, click on the right arrow (Demote) button at the left end of the Outlining toolbar, and type your text. To create headings at a higher level, press ENTER, click on the left arrow (Promote) button at the left end of the Outlining toolbar, and type your text. You can also use the button with the double arrowhead (Demote to Body Text) to create body text.

5. Continue selecting heading levels and creating your outline as just described.

Mouse Shortcuts:

   Switches to Outline view

   Promotes a heading

   Demotes a heading

   Changes a heading to body text

Creates a document that you can expand and collapse in Outline view to get an overview or a close-up view of your work. You can also transform existing text into an outline by switching to Outline view and promoting and demoting headings, as described in a moment. Note that headings with subheadings underneath them have a plus sign icon to their left, while headings with no subheadings have a minus sign instead. (Body text paragraphs have a small square to their left.)

Once you've created your outline, you may need to select text within it (either headings or body text) in preparation for reworking or reorganizing it. In general, you select text in Outline view much as you do in any other view. (See SELECTING TEXT under "General Procedures.") However, there are a few selection techniques specific to Outline view:

• To select a heading without selecting any subheadings or subtext, click in the selection bar to its left.

- To select a body text paragraph, click in the selection bar to its left, or click on the body text mark to its left (a small square).

- To select a heading along with any subheadings and subtext, double-click in the selection bar to its left, or click once on the plus sign icon to its left.

Expanding and Collapsing Outlines

To collapse your document:

1. Place the insertion point within the heading whose subheads and/or subtext you wish to conceal.

2. Click on the Collapse button (the minus sign) on the Outlining toolbar or press ALT+SHIFT+MINUS SIGN. This collapses subheadings and subtext one level at time; a wide variety of other ways of collapsing your outline are listed below.

To expand your document:

1. Place the insertion point in the heading whose concealed subheads and/or subtext you wish to reveal.

2. Click on the Expand button on the Outlining toolbar or press ALT+SHIFT+PLUS SIGN. This expands subheadings and subtext one level at time; other ways of expanding your outline are listed below.

Keyboard Shortcuts

ALT+SHIFT+ PLUS SIGN	Expands subheads and subtext one level at a time
ALT+SHIFT+ MINUS SIGN	Collapses subheads and subtext one level at a time
ALT+SHIFT+ *heading level number*	Expands or collapses the outline to the designated level
ALT+SHIFT+A	Collapses or expands the entire outline
ALT+SHIFT+L	Toggles between showing first line of body text in each paragraph and showing all body text

Mouse Shortcuts:

 Expands subheads and body text under head

Collapses subheads and body text under head

 to Expand or collapse outline to designated level

 Collapses or expands entire outline

 Toggles between showing just the first line of body text in each paragraph and showing all body text

Show Formatting button removes or displays all formatting

Double-click on plus sign icon to left of heading — Alternately collapses or expands any subheadings or subtext

Permits you to "expand" and "collapse" your outline in a variety of ways—enabling you to choose how much detail you want to see in your document. A gray line beneath headings indicates that headings or text are concealed from view. If you want to see more of your document without collapsing headings or text, deselect the Show Formatting button on the Outlining toolbar; this removes font styles and larger point sizes from the heading text, permitting you to see more text at a time on the screen.

Promoting and Demoting Outline Elements

1. Make sure you're in Outline view and place the insertion point within the heading or body text to be promoted or demoted.

2. Click on the Promote button on the Outlining toolbar or press ALT+SHIFT+LEFT ARROW to promote headings or text one level at a time. Click on the Demote button on the Outlining toolbar or press ALT+SHIFT+RIGHT ARROW to demote headings one level at a time.

Promotes or demotes the designated heading or body text one heading level at a time; just repeat the preceding steps to promote or demote a heading more than a single level. If you promote body text, it changes to a heading of the same level as the heading just above it. To demote a heading to body text, click on the Demote to Body Text button on the Outlining toolbar. You can also select multiple headings and demote or promote them all at once if you want to demote or promote them by the same amount.

Another way to promote or demote headings and body text is to drag on the associated icons to their left. Dragging on a plus sign icon promotes or demotes both that heading and all the associated subheadings and subtext; dragging on a minus sign icon or body text symbol promotes or demotes that element only. As you drag to the left or right, a vertical line indicates where the outline elements will be positioned when you release the mouse button.

Keyboard Shortcuts:

ALT+SHIFT+LEFT ARROW   Promotes heading to next higher level

ALT+SHIFT+RIGHT ARROW   Demotes heading to next lower level

Mouse Shortcuts

 Promotes heading to next higher level

 Demotes heading to next lower level

 Demotes heading to body text

Rearranging Your Outline

1. Make sure you're in Outline view and place the insertion point within the heading or body text paragraph to be moved.

2. Click on the Move Up button on the Outlining toolbar or press ALT+SHIFT+UP ARROW to move up the designated element up one line at a time. Click on the Move Down button on the Outlining toolbar or press ALT+SHIFT+DOWN ARROW to move the designated element down one line at a time.

Moves the selected text or heading up or down one line
at a time. To move more than a single heading or body
text paragraph, first select the elements to be moved and
then follow the steps just outlined.

Another way to move headings and body text is to drag
on the associated icons to their left. Dragging on a plus
sign icon moves both that heading and all the associated
subheadings and subtext; dragging on a minus sign icon
or body text symbol moves that element only. As you drag
up or down, a horizontal line indicates where the outline
elements will be positioned when you release the mouse
button.

Keyboard Shortcuts:

ALT+SHIFT+UP ARROW   Moves heading up one line at a
                            time

ALT+SHIFT+DOWN ARROW   Moves heading down one line at a
                            time

Mouse Shortcuts:

⬆   Moves heading up one line at a time

⬇   Moves heading down one line at a time

OVERTYPE MODE

1. Press the INS key or double-click on the OVR indicator at
   the bottom of the screen.

Turns on overtype mode, if it's not already on; turns it off
if it's on. (You know overtype mode is on if the OVR
indicator at the bottom of the screen is black.) In overtype
mode, text that you type overwrites existing text instead
of pushing it to the right. (Overtype mode is off by
default.) Note that you can use the INS key instead of
CTRL+V to paste the contents of the Clipboard into your
document, in which case INS does not toggle overtype
mode on and off. See "Edit" under OPTIONS for details.
Also see INSERT MODE.

PAGE BREAKS

1. Place the insertion point where you want to end one page and begin another.

2. Choose Insert, Break.

3. Make sure Page Break is selected, and click on OK or press ENTER.

Keyboard Shortcut:

CTRL+ENTER   Inserts manual page break

Inserts a *hard* (or *manual*) *page break* into your document, telling Word to move to the next page regardless of whether the current page has filled with text. (In contrast, Word enters *soft,* or *automatic, page breaks* when it fills one page and needs to move on to another. This type of page break can change position if you add or remove text from your document.) In Normal view, page break characters show up as a horizontal line with the words "Page Break" in the middle. To get rid of a hard page break, make sure you're in Normal view, place the insertion point directly over the page break, and press DEL.

You can set some general guidelines for page breaks by issuing the Format, Paragraph command, selecting the Text Flow tab, and making selections under Pagination. Selecting Widow/Orphan Control prohibits the display of just one word on the very last line of a paragraph or just one line of a paragraph at the very top or bottom of a page. Selecting Keep Lines Together keeps Word from breaking the designated paragraph. Selecting the Keep with Next check box prevents Word from inserting a page break between the designated paragraph and the subsequent paragraph. And selecting Page Break Before ensures that a page break occurs before a specific item—a heading that should always appear on a new page, for example.

PAGE SETUP

See ALIGNMENT, HEADERS AND FOOTERS, LINE
NUMBERS, MARGINS, PAPER SIZE AND SOURCE,
and SECTIONS.

PAGINATION

1. Choose Insert, Page Numbers.
2. Under Position, choose where to place page numbers.
3. Under Alignment, choose how to align page numbers.
4. Click on OK or press ENTER.

Paginates your entire document, automatically placing
page numbers either in headers or in footers. Note that
you can also insert page numbers with the Header and
Footer command if you prefer. (See HEADERS AND
FOOTERS.) Deselect the Show Number on First Page
check box to have Word paginate the entire document but
conceal the page number on the first page. Page numbers
only show up in Page Layout view or Print Preview.

To create a custom page numbering style, choose the
Format button in the Page Numbers dialog box. Then you
can select a different number format, choose to include
chapter numbers, decide to have page numbers resume
where those in the previous section left off, and pick a
specific starting page number for the current section.

To remove page numbers, open the header or footer area
and delete the page number within it. This will eliminate
all page numbers unless you created different headers
and footers for different areas in your document.

PAPER SIZE AND SOURCE

1. Choose File, Page Setup.
2. Choose the Paper Size or Paper Source tab.
3. Make the desired selections.
4. Click on OK or press ENTER.

Lets you determine the size of paper to print on, its orientation, and its source (which printer tray it will come from).

On the Paper Size tab, you can choose a preset size of paper under Paper Size, or you can specify custom measurements under Width and Height. Under Orientation, you can choose Portrait to orient the page vertically and Landscape to orient the page horizontally. If you switch between landscape and portrait modes, Word switches the Top/Bottom and Left/Right margins. For example, if you have top and bottom margins of 1 inch and right and left margins of 2 inches in portrait mode and you switch to landscape mode, you'll have left and right margins of 1 inch and top and bottom margins of 2 inches.

On the Paper Source tab, First Page lets you choose the source of the first piece of paper used to print your document. Other Pages lets you choose the paper source for all subsequent pages in your document. Typically, you'll print all pages on the same type of paper from the same source. However, in certain cases—as when using letterhead for the first page of a letter—it's nice to be able to select a different paper source for the first page.

Under Apply To on both the Paper Size and Paper Source tabs, you can choose which portion of document to affect. You can also make selections on either tab and then choose the Default button to make those settings into the defaults for the active template.

PARAGRAPH FORMATTING

Word stores all types of paragraph formatting—including alignment, indentation, and tabs—in the paragraph marks that it inserts at the end of each paragraph. (You can click on the Show/Hide button on the Standard toolbar to display paragraph marks on the screen.) Note that Word inserts a paragraph mark each time you press ENTER, and considers any amount of text followed by a paragraph mark to be a separate paragraph.

You can copy paragraph formatting by copying a paragraph marker from the end of the paragraph whose formatting you want to copy to just past the last

character in the paragraph you want to format. (See
COPYING TEXT AND GRAPHICS and DRAG AND DROP.)
When you move or copy paragraphs, *make sure* to include
the paragraph mark if you want to retain the paragraph
formatting, and make sure *not* to include the paragraph
mark if you want the moved or copied text to take on the
paragraph formatting of the new location.

Mouse Shortcut:

 Displays or hides paragraph marks, as well as other
hidden text characters

PASSWORDS

1. Open or create the document to be protected with a
   password.

2. Choose File, Save As and type a name for your
   document under File Name, if necessary.

3. Choose the Options button.

4. Type a password under Protection Password or Write
   Reservation Password. (Passwords can be up to 15
   characters and are case sensitive.)

5. Click on OK or press ENTER.

6. When prompted, retype the password for confirmation
   and then click on OK or press ENTER.

7. Click on OK or press ENTER to save password protection
   with your document.

Assigns a password to the active document, so only users
with the password can open it in the future. *Make sure to
record your password*. Without it, you can't gain access
to the password-protected document. Keep in mind that
passwords prevent files from being read by unauthorized
users, but do not protect files against deletion. See also
OPENING FILES, PROTECTING DOCUMENTS, and
SAVE AS.

If you enter a password under Protection Password, no
one can open the document without first supplying the
password. If you enter a password under Write
Reservation Password, only those who know the
password can open the document normally. Users who
don't know the password can open the document as
read-only, so they can read it but not make any changes

to it. To provide minimal protection for a document, you can select the Read-Only Recommended check box. In this case, Word always suggests that you open the document as read-only, but does not prevent you from opening the document normally.

To change or eliminate passwords, open the file to which you assigned the password (you'll need the password to do this). Then issue the File, Save As command and select the Options button. Select the existing password under either Protection Password or Write Reservation Password (it will look like a series of asterisks), and then either type a new password or press DEL to delete the password and unprotect the file. Finally, resave the file. You can also turn off the read-only recommended message associated with a file just by deselecting the Read-Only Recommended check box and resaving the file. (You can't do this if you opened the file as read-only.)

PASTE

See COPYING TEXT AND GRAPHICS and CUT AND PASTE.

PASTE SPECIAL

See EMBEDDING and LINKING.

PICTURE

See GRAPHICS.

PRINTING

1. Choose File, Print.
2. From the Print What drop-down list box, choose what you want to print.
3. Under Copies, choose how many copies of the document to print.
4. Under Page Range, choose which portion of the document to print.

5. Under Print, choose whether to print all pages, or just even or odd pages.

6. Click on OK or press ENTER.

Keyboard Shortcut:
CTRL+P   Displays the Print dialog box

Mouse Shortcut:

   Prints the current document

Prints your document's text, summary information, annotations, and so forth. To print the document's text along with either summary information or annotations, choose the Options button and proceed from there. See "Print" under OPTIONS. See also ENVELOPES, LABELS, PAPER SIZE AND SOURCE, and PRINT PREVIEW.

Under Page Range, choose whether to print the entire document (All), the page you're on (Current Page), or a selected range of pages (Pages). If you've selected any portion of your document, you can also choose Selection to print just the selected material.

Choose the Printer button if you need to select a new printer. (The current printer is listed at the top of the Print dialog box.) Choose Set as Default Printer in the Print Setup dialog box to establish the new printer as the default printer. (If the printer you want isn't listed, refer to your Windows documentation.)

Select the Print to File check box to "print" to a file rather than a printer. This enables you to print from another computer or from a computer that does not have Word for Windows installed. First choose the desired printer in the Print dialog box. Then select Print to File and click on OK. Word displays the Print to File dialog box, in which you enter a file name and choose where to store the file.

PRINT PREVIEW

1. Open the document you want to preview.

2. If necessary, move to the page that you want to preview.

3. Choose File, Print Preview.

Keyboard Shortcut:
CTRL+F2   Displays the Print Preview screen

Mouse Shortcuts:

    Displays the Print Preview screen

    Prints the current document from within
Print Preview

    The Magnifier; lets you magnify a designated
portion of the document for viewing or editing

    Displays a single page

    Displays multiple pages

    The Zoom Control button; lets you zoom in or
out to enlarge or reduce the display

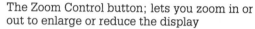   Displays or hides the vertical and horizontal
rulers

    Shrinks the document to fit on fewer pages, if
possible

    Displays or turns off full screen view, with
    only document pages and the Print Preview
toolbar displayed

Displays a preview of how your document will appear
when printed. Using the Print Preview toolbar buttons
listed above, you can display multiple pages, view a
specified area of the document in greater detail, zoom
in and out, switch to full screen view, and print your
document.

Shrink to Fit enables you to print using fewer pages if
possible; if your document contains very little text on the
last page, Word will "shrink" the document as a whole so
that that text can be printed on the previous page.

To edit in the Print Preview screen, make sure the
Magnifer button is selected and point to the text area to
be edited (the mouse pointer should change to a
magnifying glass). Click to magnify the area of the
document you click on. Next click on the Magnifier button
to deselect it; the mouse pointer returns to normal and
you can go ahead and edit. When you're done editing,
click on the Magnifier button once again and click within
the document to return it to its original size.

When you're done previewing your document, click on the Close button on the Print Preview toolbar or press ESC to return to the normal editing screen. Or, select a view button in the lower-left corner of the screen.

PROTECTING DOCUMENTS

1. Open the document to be protected.
2. Choose Tools, Protect Document.
3. Under Protect Document For, choose either Revisions, Annotations, or Forms.
4. If you like, enter a password of up to 15 characters under Password.
5. Click on OK or press ENTER.

Permits you to protect documents from all but certain types of changes. If you select Revisions, changes to the document will show up as revision marks (see REVISIONS). If you select Annotations, users can open and annotate the document but cannot make changes to the document itself (see ANNOTATIONS). Selecting Forms protects all but a document's form fields from changes. You can also choose the Sections button to determine which sections of your form to protect, if applicable. (See FORMS.)

It's a good idea to enter a password to prevent unauthorized users from unprotecting your documents. (This protects your documents against being unprotected, *not* against being opened. See PASSWORDS for details on how to protect your documents from being opened or revised by others.) After entering a password, press ENTER and then type it again for confirmation. Your password is case sensitive, and you cannot unprotect your document without it (that is to say, you should record it somewhere safe).

To unprotect protected documents, just choose Unprotect Document from the Tools menu. Remember, you must have the password to unprotect any document that has been password-protected.

READ-ONLY FILES

See OPENING FILES, "Save" under OPTIONS, and PASSWORDS.

REDO

1. Choose <u>E</u>dit, <u>R</u>edo.

Keyboard Shortcut:

F4   Reverses the previous undo operations

Mouse Shortcut:

    Reverses the previous undo operations

Lets you reverse the effects of one or more previous undo operations. This command is only available if you have performed an undo operation (see UNDO). If not, the command name changes to <u>R</u>epeat (see REPEAT). The complete command name changes depending on the operation being redone—it might be <u>R</u>edo Bold, for example.

You can reverse several undo operations, not just the most recent one. For example, if you undid boldfacing and then undid some typing, you could redo both the typing and the boldfacing operations, in that order, by choosing the <u>R</u>edo command from the <u>E</u>dit menu twice. (Note that operations are undone in reverse order from the order in which they were performed.) You can also select the Redo button repeatedly, or click on the downward-pointing arrow to its right and choose one or more actions to redo from the list that appears.

REPEAT

1. Perform an action such as typing or formatting.
2. If necessary, select the text or other item on which to perform the repeated action.
3. Choose <u>E</u>dit, <u>R</u>epeat.

Keyboard Shortcut:

F4   Repeats the previous action

Repeats your last action, if possible. The complete command name changes depending on the operation being repeated—examples are Repeat Typing or Repeat Bold. If your most recent action was an undo operation, this command name changes to Redo (see REDO).

You can repeat your most recent action multiple times. For instance, if your last action was to apply a border to some text, you can continue to select text and place a border around it by choosing Edit, Repeat or by pressing F4.

REPLACING TEXT, FORMATTING, AND SPECIAL CHARACTERS

1. Choose Edit, Replace.
2. Under Find What, enter the text, formatting, or special characters to be found.
3. Under Replace With, enter the text, formatting, or special characters to replace it with.
4. Under Search, choose whether to search forward (Down), backward (Up), or through the entire document (All).
5. Click on Find Next or press ENTER to hunt for the designated search string.
6. Choose Replace to remove the search string that you've found, insert its designated replacement, and move on to the next instance of the search string, if there is one. Choose Replace All to replace all instances of the search string. Or, choose Find Next again to move on to the next occurrence of the search string, without changing the current one.
7. Choose Close or Cancel to close the Replace dialog box when you're done with the search and replace operation.

Keyboard Shortcut:

CTRL+H   Displays the Replace dialog box

Finds the next instance of the specified text, formatting, or special character and replaces it with the designated replacement string. If you've searched for and replaced several items during the current work session, they are listed in the Find What and Replace With drop-down list boxes. To repeat a particular search or replace, just pull down the list box and pick the item to be searched for or replaced.

You can perform a replace operation in only a portion of your document by selecting that text before issuing the Replace command. You can also refine your search by choosing the Match Case, Find Whole Words Only, Use Pattern Matching, and Sounds Like check boxes. If you select Match Case, Word only finds text strings that exactly match those that you enter under Find What. For example, if you enter diaphanous under Find What, Word will find "diaphanous" but not "DIAPHANOUS" or "Diaphanous." And if you choose Find Whole Words Only, Word only finds complete words that match the text string. For example, if you enter elf in the Find What text box, Word will find "elf" but will not find "selfishness" or "self-centered." If you select Use Pattern Matching, you can include special search operators in the Find What text box. For instance, you can use the ? operator to represent any single character, so a text string of br?w will find "brew" and "brow." Consult your Word documentation or the on-line help system for a list of all available search operators. Lastly, if you select the Sounds Like check box, Word tracks down words that sound similar to the text string but are spelled differently.

You can also search for and replace formatting and special characters. First place the insertion point in either the Find What or Replace With text box. Then, to search for formatting, choose the Format button in the Replace dialog box. Select Font to look for particular font characteristics, Paragraph to search for paragraph formatting, Language to track down text in a particular language, and Style to hunt for a specific style. The selections you make are displayed in the Format boxes directly underneath the Find What and Replace With text boxes. Although you can look for a text string with the designated format, you can also search for a format alone by leaving the Find What box blank. To clear any selected formatting, choose the No Formatting button.

To look for and replace special characters, first place the insertion point in either the Find What or Replace With text box. Then choose the Special button and make a selection from the menu that appears. This inserts a special code representing the character in the Find What or Replace With text box. At this point you can go ahead and perform the replace operation, as described above.

REVISIONS

Word permits you to add revision marks when you make changes or additions to a document. This lets you keep track of any changes as well as to accept or reject them. Word can even indicate that several people are reviewing a single document by using different colored revision marks.

You can protect documents so that anyone altering them can only make changes in the form of revision marks. This assures that you can keep tabs on any changes. (See PROTECTING DOCUMENTS.) You can also customize revision marks (see "Revisions" under OPTIONS).

Adding Revision Marks

1. Open the document to be revised.
2. Choose Tools, Revisions.
3. Select the Mark Revisions While Editing check box.
4. Click on OK or press ENTER.

Mouse Shortcut:

Double-click on MRK indicator at bottom of screen	Opens Revisions dialog box

Enables you to record editing changes to a document as revision marks that let others see what changes were made. By default, added text is underlined and displayed in a different shade or color, and deleted text is changed to strikethrough text and is displayed in a different shade or color. Text that has been moved is marked as strikethrough in its original location and is underlined in its new location. Finally, lines of text containing any revisions are marked with a black vertical bar to their left.

To remove revision marks from the screen, deselect the Show Revisions on Screen check box in the Revisions dialog box. If you don't want the revision marks to print, deselect the Show Revisions in Printed Document check box. In either case, Word still keeps track of revisions, but does not display them at the moment.

To customize revision marks, choose the Options button
in the Revisions dialog box and make selections from the
Options dialog box. (See "Revisions" under OPTIONS.)

If you no longer want to mark revisions in the document,
choose Tools, Revisions and deselect the Mark Revisions
While Editing check box. This doesn't remove existing
revision marks, but ensures that no further changes
are marked.

Comparing Document Versions

1. Open the edited version of the document.
2. Choose Tools, Revisions.
3. Choose Compare Versions.
4. Under Original File Name, specify the name of the
   original file that you want to compare the edited file
   with. If necessary, make selections under List Files of
   Type, Directories, and Drives.
5. Click on OK or press ENTER.

Enables you to compare an edited version and an original
version of a document. Both versions must be saved, and
must have different names. Word inserts revision marks
in the edited version of the document, indicating where
changes have taken place. To accept or reject any of
these changes, see "Reviewing Revisions."

Merging Revisions and Annotations into the Original Document

1. Open the document containing revisions and/or
   annotations.
2. Choose Tools, Revisions.
3. Select the Merge Revisions button.
4. Under Original File Name, specify the name of the
   original file into which you wish to merge revisions and
   annotations. If necessary, make selections under List
   Files of Type, Directories, and Drives.
5. Click on OK or press ENTER.

Incorporates (merges) the revision marks and annotations
in the edited version of the document into the original
version. After the operation is completed, Word displays
the original file—complete with all annotations and
revision marks from the other copy of the file.

Reviewing Revisions

1. Open the document containing the revisions to be reviewed.

2. Choose Tools, Revisions or double-click on the MRK indicator at the bottom of the screen.

3. Choose the Review button.

4. Use the two Find buttons to select the desired revisions.

5. Choose Accept to incorporate a suggested revision, Reject to discard it, or a Find button to move to the next or previous revision without making a change.

6. When you're done reviewing revisions, choose Close to return to your document.

Lets you review the revisions to your document, either accepting or rejecting them. If you decide against the last change that you made, choose the Undo Last button.

To have Word move automatically to the next revision after you accept or reject a change, select the Find Next After Accept/Reject check box. You can also move through the document by scrolling, and can select revisions with normal text selection methods. You may also want to click on the Hide Marks button to see how the document would look if you accepted all revisions. To accept or refuse all revisions at once, you can choose either the Accept All or Reject All button from the Revisions dialog box.

RULER

1. Choose View, Ruler.

Displays or hides the horizontal ruler at the top of the document window and the vertical ruler displayed in Page Layout view and Print Preview. If the Ruler option on the View menu is selected (has a check mark to its left) but the vertical ruler doesn't appear in Page Layout view, switch to Page Layout view if necessary, choose Tools, Options, choose the View tab, and select the Vertical Ruler check box.

The horizontal ruler displays the tab, indent, and margin settings for the paragraph containing the insertion point. You can use the ruler to change the left and right margins, indents, column widths, and tab stops of the paragraph containing the insertion point or of the selected paragraphs. You can use the vertical ruler to change the top and bottom margins, and the height of table rows. (See COLUMNS, INDENTATION, MARGINS, TABLES, and TABS.)

Inches are the ruler's default unit of measurement. You can change the unit of measurement by issuing the Tools, Options command, selecting the General tab, and choosing a different unit of measurement from the Measurement Units drop-down list box.

SAVE

1. Choose File, Save.

Keyboard Shortcut:

CTRL+S   Saves the active document with the same name

Mouse Shortcut:

    Saves the active document with the same name

Saves the active document or template without changing its name. You can use this command to save changes to documents that have already been saved. This automatically overwrites the old copy of the file with the new version. To retain both the old and new versions, you can give the revised file a new name with the File, Save As command. You cannot save files that have been opened as read-only. You can, however, save them under a different name with the File, Save As command. See SAVE AS and "Saving Files" under "General Procedures."

To ensure that your document is saved periodically, you can instruct Word to save it automatically at a regular interval. For details see "Save" under OPTIONS.

SAVE ALL

1. Choose File, Save All.

Saves changes to any files or templates that you have open. If any of the open files have not yet been saved,

Word opens the Save As dialog box to request a file name. Specify a file name and click on OK or press ENTER. (See the next section for details.)

SAVE AS

1. Choose File, Save As.
2. Under File Name, type a name for the file.
3. If necessary, choose a different drive and/or directory on which to save the file.
4. Click on OK or press ENTER.

Keyboard Shortcut:
CTRL+S   Opens the Save As dialog box (if you're saving a file for the first time)

Mouse Shortcut:

    Opens the Save As dialog box (if you're saving a file for the first time)

Allows you to name documents that you're saving for the first time, and to make copies of existing documents by giving them new names and/or saving them in a different location.

Under File Name, type a file name of up to eight characters. (Word will generally add the .DOC extension for you.) File names can include numbers, letters, and certain special characters such as %, −, and @, but cannot include spaces. Although files are automatically saved on the current drive and directory, you can save them on a drive and/or directory other than the default by changing the Directories and Drives settings in the Save As dialog box. Under Directories, double-click on a directory name to display all of its subdirectories and list all files it contains under File Name. (The file names are grayed because you cannot select them.) If you double-click on a directory that has no subdirectories, Word simply displays all files from that directory. You can also change the directory into which Word saves files by default (see DIRECTORIES).

The Options button in the Save As dialog box enables you to customize certain Save settings (see "Save" under OPTIONS). Also see PASSWORDS for details on protecting files by saving them with passwords.

Saving Files in Other File Formats

1. Open the file to be saved.
2. Choose File, Save As.
3. Specify a file name, and, if necessary, a different drive and/or directory in which to save the file.
4. Pull down the Save File as Type drop-down list box and choose a file format.
5. Click on OK or press ENTER.
6. When you close the document or exit Word, choose Yes to confirm that you want to save changes to the document, and then choose the desired format from the Save Format dialog box.

Enables you to save files in different formats so that they can be read by earlier versions of Word or by other applications. For example, you can save a file so that it can be read in WordPerfect 5.1. You can also save files in certain text-only formats, such as Text Only or MS-DOS Text (or ASCII) that strip away all formatting. Use these formats only if the application you're transferring material to cannot interpret any other available format. For additional information on using different file formats, consult your Word for Windows documentation or on-line help.

SECTIONS

Word enables you to divide documents into any number of *sections* so that you can format different parts of your document in different ways. This lets you use a different number of columns in different areas of the same document or set up different margins in different areas of your document, among other things. You can make sections as long or as short as you like, and you can have new sections start on the current page, on a new page, or on the next odd or even page.

By default, Word documents consist of a single section. This means that particular types of formatting—including pagination, columns, page size and orientation, and headers and footers—are applied to the entire document automatically. In certain operations, Word creates new sections (by inserting *section breaks*) automatically, such as when you compile an index and insert it within your document. In other cases, you must insert section breaks yourself, as described in a moment. If you're in Normal view, section breaks are displayed as dotted double lines and include the words "End of Section."

Deleting Section Breaks

1. Switch to Normal view, if necessary.
2. Place the insertion point on the section break line.
3. Press DEL.

Removes the designated section break. Since section breaks store the page-level formatting information for the section above them, this may also remove formatting from that material, which will then take on the formatting of the section below.

Inserting Section Breaks

1. Place the insertion point where you want the new section to begin.
2. Choose Insert, Break.
3. Under Section Breaks, choose where you want the next section to begin.
4. Click on OK or press ENTER.

Inserts a section break in the designated location and places the insertion point within the new section. If you choose Next Page, Word starts the new section on the next page. If you choose Continuous, the new section begins in the current location. If you choose Even Page or Odd Page, the new section begins on the next even- or odd-numbered page, respectively.

SELECT ALL

1. Choose Edit, Select All.

Keyboard Shortcut:

CTRL+A   Selects entire document

Mouse Shortcut:
CTRL+click or triple-click   Selects entire document
in selection bar

Selects all of the text in the active document. This feature
is useful if you need to perform an action—such as a font
change—that you want to affect the entire document.
Also see "Selecting Text" under "General Procedures."

SHADING

1. Select the paragraphs, table cells, or frame to be shaded.
2. Choose Format, Borders and Shading.
3. If necessary, choose the Shading tab.
4. Under Shading, choose a shading percentage or a fill
   pattern.
5. Click on OK or press ENTER.

Mouse Shortcuts:

                   Displays the Borders toolbar

   Enables you to apply or remove
                                       shading and fill patterns

Applies shading or a fill pattern to the designated
paragraphs, table cells, or frame. (You cannot shade
imported graphics.) Since Word considers a paragraph to
be any amount of text followed by a paragraph mark, you
can shade small bits of text by following them with a
paragraph mark (press ENTER). Text shading extends from
the left to the right indents. To make the shading fit more
closely around the shaded text, reduce the indents (see
INDENTATION). You can produce a "reverse video" text
effect if you apply a dark enough shading (80% or above),
since Word will automatically change the text color to
white so it shows up against the dark background.

Click on the Borders button on the Formatting toolbar, or
choose Show Toolbar in the Borders and Shading dialog
box to display the Borders toolbar, which includes a
shading drop-down list box.

You can also create color shading and fill patterns. First
select the desired shading percentage or fill pattern
under Shading in the Borders and Shading dialog box.
Then make choices from the Foreground and Background
drop-down list boxes.

SORTING FILES

1. Choose File, Find File and, if necessary, use the Search feature to display the desired list of files under Listed Files (see FINDING FILES).
2. Click on the Commands button and choose Sorting.
3. Under Sort Files By, choose the desired type of sort.
4. Under List Files By, choose whether to list sorted files by file name or by title.
5. Click on OK or press ENTER.

Sorts the files under Listed Files into the specified order within each directory. If you sort files by title rather than by file name, Word uses the title that you entered into the Summary Info dialog box (see SUMMARY INFO).

SORTING TEXT

1. Select the table rows, paragraphs, or list items to be sorted.
2. Choose Table, Sort. (The command name changes to Sort Text if you've selected paragraphs or list items.)
3. Under Sort By, select Paragraphs, choose a column number, or choose a field name or number.
4. Under Type, choose which kind of information to sort.
5. Choose either Ascending or Descending to determine the sort order.
6. Click on OK or press ENTER.

Sorts the selected items into the order that you specified. If you sort a numbered list, Word renumbers the list automatically. If you decide to reverse the sort operation, just click on the Undo button (see UNDO).

Under Sort By, choose Paragraphs to sort paragraphs or lists (unless you've set up fields, as described in a moment). Choose one of the column selections if you're sorting a table. Under Type, choose Text to sort by any and all characters, including letters, numbers, and symbols. Choose Number to have Word sort by numbers, ignoring other characters. Choose Date to have Word sort by date. If you select Ascending, Word sorts in ascending order—that is, from A to Z, from lower to higher numbers, and from earlier to later dates. If you select Descending, Word sorts in descending order—from Z to A, from higher to lower numbers, and from most recent (latest) to earliest dates. To exclude a list heading from the sort operation, select the Header Row option under My List Has.

If you're sorting a table, or if you lay out the data in your document in a series of "fields," Word enables you to sort by up to three different criteria at once. For example, if you're sorting a table, you can choose to sort by Column 1, and then, under Then By, indicate that you want to conduct a subsidiary sort on another column. You can even specify a third criteria in the Then By box at the bottom of the Sort dialog box. To perform such multiple criteria sorts on data that is not within a table, first lay out the data as a series of "fields" separated by tabs or commas. Then sort these fields of data much as you would sort table columns, as just described.

SPACING

Word permits you to add or remove space between characters, alter the spacing between lines, and modify the amount of space that appears between paragraphs.

Character Spacing

1. Select the text to be affected.
2. Choose Format, Font.
3. If necessary, choose the Character Spacing tab.
4. Pull down the Spacing drop-down list box and make a selection from the list.
5. Click on OK or press ENTER.

Changes the spacing between characters in your text. You can choose Expanded to include more space between characters, Condensed to reduce the space between characters, or Normal to return character spacing to normal. When you choose either Expanded or Condensed, the By setting defaults to 1 point. You can change that amount to modify the character spacing of selected text.

You can also choose the Kerning for Fonts check box to have Word *kern* your text—that is, selectively reduce the space between certain pairs of letters (such as "A" and "W") to improve the way they look. (This is different from the Spacing options, which affect the amount of space between *all* characters.) In the Points and Above text box, choose which point sizes you want affected.

Line Spacing

1. Select the paragraphs to be affected.
2. Choose Format, Paragraph.
3. Make sure the Indents and Spacing tab is selected.
4. Choose the desired selection in the Line Spacing drop-down list box.
5. Click on OK or press ENTER.

Keyboard Shortcuts:

CTRL+1   Applies single-spacing to the current paragraph or the selected text

CTRL+2   Applies double-spacing to the current paragraph or the selected text

CTRL+5   Applies 1.5 spacing to the current paragraph or the selected text

Applies the designated line spacing to the selected text. In general, the amount of space between lines depends on the size of the font you're using. You can also choose At Least in the Line Spacing drop-down list box to have Word set a minimum spacing that it can go above but not below, and you can choose Exactly to specify the exact space between lines (this setting won't change even if you switch to a different font style or point size). Finally, you can choose Multiple to set a custom line spacing, such as 2.5 lines.

Paragraph Spacing

1. Select the paragraphs to be affected.
2. Choose Format, Paragraph.
3. Make sure the Indents and Spacing tab is selected.
4. Under Before or After, choose how much space you want to appear before or after each paragraph.
5. Click on OK or press ENTER.

Determines the amount of space between paragraphs. If you enter values under both Before and After, Word combines them, producing a larger amount of space between paragraphs. If you prefer to indent the beginning of each paragraph, rather than including space between paragraphs, see INDENTATION.

SPELL CHECKING

1. Open the document whose spelling you want to check.

2. Choose Tools, Spelling.

3. If Word finds a word that is not in its dictionary, it highlights the word in your document and displays it under Not in Dictionary in the Spelling dialog box. Choose Change to accept the suggested correction under Change To, or choose Ignore to leave the word unchanged.

4. Word moves on to any additional words that aren't in its dictionary; again correct or bypass these words.

5. When the spell check is completed, click on OK or press ENTER to go back to your document.

Keyboard Shortcut:

F7   Initiates a spell check and displays the Spelling dialog box

Mouse Shortcut:

      Initiates a spell check and displays the Spelling dialog box

Checks the spelling of your entire document. Place the insertion point where you want the spell check to begin. You can also check just a portion of your document by selecting it before initiating the spell check.

In the Spelling dialog box, you also have the option of editing the text under Change To or choosing another alternative from the list of possible changes under Suggestions. And you can delete words from your document by first deleting the contents of the Change To box and then choosing the Delete button (it will replace the Change button). Choose Change All to correct a particular spelling error throughout your document (this button changes to Delete All when you erase the contents of the Change To box). Choose AutoCorrect to add common typing errors, and their corrections, to your

AutoCorrect list so Word can fix them automatically as you type (see AUTOCORRECT).

If Word stops on a word that is not a misspelling—such as a proper name or a technical term—choose the Ignore button to bypass the word without changing it, or choose Ignore All to bypass the word for the remainder of the current work session. You can also choose the Add button to add a word to the custom dictionary specified under Add Words To. (See the next section.) Choose Undo Last to reverse the most recent correction. Choose the Suggest button to display a list of suggestions in the Suggestions box. (This option is only available if you tell Word not display suggestions; see "Spelling" under OPTIONS.) Finally, choose Options if you want to customize how the spell check takes place. (Also see "Spelling" under OPTIONS.)

Word bases its spell check on the language or languages selected for the current document. To check the spelling of text in another language, install the appropriate dictionary and inform Word which text is in what language. (See LANGUAGE.)

Using Custom Dictionaries

To add words to a custom dictionary during a spell check:

1. Initiate the spell check, as just described.
2. Check that the custom dictionary you want to use is listed under Add Words To.
3. When the desired word is listed under Not in Dictionary, choose the Add button.

Adds the designated word to the custom dictionary listed under Add Words To, keeping Word from stopping on that word during future spell checks. (Custom dictionaries must be open to be used in spell checks, as described in a moment.) CUSTOM.DIC is Word's default custom dictionary, and is open by default when you run a spell check. In addition, you can create your own custom dictionaries, as described next.

To create additional custom dictionaries:

1. Choose Tools, Options.
2. Choose the Spelling tab, if necessary.
3. Choose New under Custom Dictionaries.

4. Under File <u>N</u>ame, specify a file name for the dictionary and click on OK or press ENTER. Choose OK again to leave the Options dialog box.

Creates a new custom dictionary to which you can add words that you want Word to bypass during spell checks. Word adds the name of the new custom dictionary to the Custom <u>D</u>ictionaries list box, placing a selected check box to its left. This means that the new dictionary file will show up under Add <u>W</u>ords To in the Spelling dialog box, and you can select it to add words to it. If the check box is not selected, Word will not use the custom dictionary, as described next.

To open or close custom dictionaries:

1. Choose <u>T</u>ools, <u>O</u>ptions.
2. If necessary, choose the Spelling tab.
3. Under Custom <u>D</u>ictionaries, select the check boxes for the custom dictionaries that you want to use during spell checks, and deselect the check boxes for those that you do not want to use.
4. Click on OK or press ENTER.

Opens (selected check box) or closes (deselected check box) the designated custom dictionary. Closing a custom dictionary instructs Word not to use it during spell checks. Word uses all open dictionaries (up to ten) during spell checks.

To edit a custom dictionary:

1. Choose <u>T</u>ools, <u>O</u>ptions.
2. Choose the Spelling tab, if necessary.
3. Under Custom <u>D</u>ictionaries, select the dictionary to be edited, choose <u>E</u>dit, choose <u>Y</u>es to continue, and then choose OK to close the Options dialog box.
4. Edit the displayed dictionary. You can delete words, and can add words by typing them on a line of their own and pressing ENTER.
5. Choose <u>F</u>ile, <u>S</u>ave to save the dictionary.
6. Choose <u>F</u>ile, <u>C</u>lose to close the dictionary file.

Enables you to make multiple additions or deletions to the open dictionary file.

To add and remove custom dictionaries:

1. Choose Tools, Options.
2. Choose the Spelling tab, if necessary.
3. Select the dictionary to be removed and then click on the Remove button. Or, choose the Add button and specify the name of the dictionary to add in the Add Custom Dictionary dialog box.
4. Click on OK or press ENTER.

SPIKE

To move items onto the Spike:

1. Select the text, table, or graphic you want to place on the Spike.
2. Press CTRL+F3.
3. Repeat steps 1 and 2 as often as you like. Existing material on the Spike will not be replaced by new items that you add.

To insert everything from the Spike into a designated location:

1. Place the insertion point where you want to insert all the material that you've accumulated on the Spike.
2. Press CTRL+SHIFT+F3.

Allows you to cut and paste several items at a time. (You can move but cannot copy text or graphics using the Spike.) Unlike the Clipboard, the Spike doesn't discard its previous contents when you add something new. Inserting the Spike's contents into your document with CTRL+SHIFT+F3 clears the Spike. To insert the Spike's contents without emptying out the Spike, instead type spike and then press F3. See also CLIPBOARD and CUT AND PASTE.

STRIKETHROUGH

1. Choose the text to be affected.
2. Choose Format, Font.
3. If necessary, choose the Font tab.
4. Under Effects, select the Strikethrough check box.
5. Click on OK or press ENTER.

Places a horizontal line though the designated text. You can just as easily remove the strikethrough line by selecting the text, following the preceding steps, and deselecting the Strikethrough check box. Also see REVISIONS.

STYLES

Styles are named formatting combinations that you can apply in a single step. Word comes with a number of built-in styles, and you can also produce your own. (An important built-in style is the Normal style, Word's default body text style.) For example, if you frequently create centered headings in a specific font and point size, you can create a style that lets you apply all those formats at once. If you modify a style, those changes are automatically reflected in any text in the active document to which the style has been applied. You can also ask Word to apply styles automatically (see AUTOFORMAT).

There are two types of styles: characters styles and paragraph styles. Character styles can include any of the formatting attributes from the Font dialog box (choose Format, Font), plus language and dictionary settings. Paragraph styles can include all the character formats, and can incorporate paragraph-level formatting such as indentation and alignment.

Styles are saved in templates; the available styles depend upon the template in use (see TEMPLATES). Word's Style Gallery (covered shortly) enables you to see what styles are available with which templates.

Applying Styles

1. Select the text to be affected.
2. Choose Format, Style.
3. If necessary, choose a new set of styles from the List drop-down list box.
4. Under Styles, choose the desired style.
5. Click on the Apply button or press ENTER.

Keyboard Shortcuts:

CTRL+SHIFT+N	Applies the Normal style
ALT+CTRL+1	Applies the Heading 1 style

ALT+CTRL+2	Applies the Heading 2 style
ALT+CTRL+3	Applies the Heading 3 style
CTRL+SPACEBAR	Removes character styles

Mouse Shortcut:

Select a style from this drop-down list box to affect the selected text (hold down SHIFT while clicking on the downward-pointing arrow to display a complete list of styles); the bold listings are paragraph styles

Applies the designated style to the selected text. When applying character styles, select the exact amount of text to be formatted. When applying paragraph styles, place the insertion point within any single paragraph to be affected, or select at least some text in all paragraphs to be affected. You can also apply character styles with the Format Painter button on the Standard toolbar. (See FONTS.)

To assign shortcut keys to commonly used styles, choose the desired style in the Style dialog box, choose Modify, choose Shortcut Key, and then assign a shortcut key as described under CUSTOMIZE.

Creating Styles

To quickly create a paragraph style:

1. Create or select a paragraph that contains the desired formatting.
2. Select the Style drop-down list box on the Formatting toolbar.
3. Type a style name and press ENTER.

To create a paragraph or character style:

1. Choose Format, Style.
2. Choose the New button.
3. Under Name, type a name for the new style. (Style names are case sensitive, can include commas and spaces, and can be up to 253 characters long.)
4. Under Style Type, choose whether to create a paragraph style or a character style.
5. Choose the Format button and decide which formatting attributes to include in the style. (For details on the options in this menu, see FONT, TABS, and so on.)

6. When you're done selecting formatting attributes, click on OK or press ENTER to return to the New Style dialog box, and then click on OK or press ENTER to return to the Style dialog box.

7. Either define another new style using steps 3 through 6, or choose Close to return to your document.

Creates a style that you can use to format text in your document. If you want this new style to be available in all documents created using the template upon which the active document is based, choose the Add to Template check box in the New Style dialog box.

When you create a new style using the New Style dialog box, the Based On drop-down list box will list the style applied to the selected text or the text containing the insertion point. You can choose another existing style to use as a basis for the new style. You can also indicate which style should follow the style you're creating by specifying a file name under Style for Following Paragraph. This way Word automatically switches over to that style when you press ENTER.

You can delete a user-defined style (a style that you've created rather than one supplied with Word) by highlighting its name and choosing the Delete button. You can also delete, copy, and rename styles through the Organizer (see ORGANIZER).

Modifying Styles

To modify a style quickly:

1. Select some text formatted with the desired character or paragraph style.

2. Modify the selected text using normal formatting techniques.

3. Click in the Style box on the Formatting toolbar and then press ENTER.

4. Choose OK in the Reapply Style dialog box.

You can also modify styles using the Style command:

1. Choose Format, Style.

2. In the Styles list box, choose the style to be altered. (If it doesn't appear, make a new selection from the List drop-down list box.)

3. Click on the Modify button.

4. Choose Format, and then choose which aspect of the style to modify. (For details on the options in this Format menu, consult FONT, TABS, and so on.)

5. When you're done making modifications, click on OK or press ENTER to return to the Modify Style dialog box, and then click on OK or press ENTER to return to the Style dialog box.

6. Choose Close to return to your document.

Modifies the selected style as indicated. You can also modify several styles by repeating steps 2 through 4. Note that all text in the active document that is formatted with the modified style will be updated to reflect any changes to the style.

Select Add To Template in the Modify Style dialog box to have Word add the modified style to the template associated with the current document. This way the modified style will be available in new documents you base upon that template. You can also choose a style to follow the modified style by specifying a file name under Style for Following Paragraph. Then you can switch to the designated style just by pressing ENTER.

Using the Style Gallery

1. Open a document in which styles have been applied.

2. Choose Format, Style Gallery.

3. Choose the desired template under Template.

4. If you like, select options under Preview to see how the new styles will affect your document.

5. Click on OK or press ENTER.

Applies the styles from the selected template to your document. Note that this only affects your document if there are styles applied to it.

Under Preview, Document shows how the active document will look when formatted with the styles from the selected template. Example brings up an example document formatted with styles from the selected template. And Style Samples gives you a preview of all styles in the selected template. Also see TEMPLATES.

SUBSCRIPT AND SUPERSCRIPT

1. Choose the text to be affected.
2. Choose Format, Font.
3. If necessary, choose the Font tab.
4. Under Effects, select either Subscript or Superscript.
5. Click on OK or press ENTER.

Keyboard Shortcuts:

CTRL+PLUS SIGN — Changes selected text to superscript (hold down SHIFT and press the equal sign to get a plus sign) or changes superscript to normal text

CTRL+EQUAL SIGN — Changes selected text to subscript, or changes subscript to normal text

Changes the designated text into subscript (lowered) or superscript (raised) text that appears in a smaller point size. You can return sub- or superscript text to normal text by selecting it, following the preceding steps, and deselecting the Subscript or Superscript check box.

You can also raise or lower text without changing its point size. To do so, choose Format, Font, choose the Character Spacing tab if necessary, pick either Raised or Lowered from the Position drop-down list box, indicate by how much you want the text raised or lowered in the By text box, and click on OK.

SUMMARY INFO

1. Choose File, Summary Info.
2. Enter the desired summary information.
3. Click on OK or press ENTER.

Lets you enter summary information for the active document. You can use this information to find and sort files (see FINDING FILES and SORTING FILES). You can also request that Word prompt you for summary information each time you save. (See "Save" under OPTIONS.)

Under Author, Word automatically uses the name from the User Info tab on the Options dialog box. (See

OPTIONS.) Feel free to type in a new name. Under Title, Word enters the first few words in the active document, assuming that it has been saved; you'll probably want to enter a new document title. You can enter a document subject, as well as keywords and comments. These items are primarily of use when you are searching for files. Choose the Statistics button to see additional information about the active document, including the time it was created and last saved, as well as the number of pages, words, and characters it contains.

SYMBOLS

1. Choose Insert, Symbol.
2. Choose the Symbols tab, if necessary.
3. If you like, choose a different font from the Font drop-down list box.
4. Choose the desired symbol and then click on Insert or press ENTER.
5. Choose Close when you're done entering symbols.

Lets you insert symbols and other special characters into your text. You can also choose the Special Characters tab in the Symbol dialog box to insert special characters such as trademark symbols into your document. Just highlight the desired character under Character and click on Insert or press ENTER. If there's a symbol or special character that you use frequently but that has no shortcut key, you can choose Shortcut Key and create a customized shortcut key. (See CUSTOMIZE.)

TABLE OF AUTHORITIES

If you're in the legal field, you may need to create a table of authorities listing the location of the citations in your document. To do so, you first mark the citations, and then generate the table of authorities.

Marking Citations

1. Select the first instance of a citation.
2. Press ALT+SHIFT+I.

3. Under Selected Text, make any needed edits to the long citation. This is how the citation will appear in your table of authorities.

4. Under Category, choose the appropriate category for the citation.

5. Under Short Citation, enter the text to be searched for.

6. Choose Mark to mark the selected citation, or choose Mark All to mark every citation (short or long) matching the one in the Mark Citation dialog box.

7. Choose Next Citation or scroll through your document to hunt for further citations to be marked. Then choose Mark or Mark All to mark them for inclusion in the table of authorities.

8. Choose Close to close the Mark Citation dialog box.

Marks the citations in your document in preparation for generating a table of authorities.

Producing a Table of Authorities

1. Mark all the citations in your document, as described in "Marking Citations."

2. Place the insertion point where you want the table of authorities to go.

3. Choose Insert, Index and Tables.

4. If necessary, choose the Table of Authorities tab.

5. Under Category, choose which type of citation to compile.

6. Choose a style for your table of authorities under Formats.

7. Click on OK or press ENTER.

Compiles a table of authorities and places it in your document at the insertion point. This table will consist of the long version of the citation, its page number, plus the page numbers of all short versions of the citation.

If your document changes, you may need to update the table of authorities. (The table of authorities is actually a field; see FIELDS.) To do so, place the insertion point anywhere in the table of authorities and press F9. Then either update page numbers only, or update the entire table of authorities (choose this option if you've added any new citations).

TABLE OF CONTENTS

1. Make sure that Word's built-in heading styles are applied to the headings in your document (see STYLES).
2. Place the insertion point where you want the table of contents to go.
3. Choose Insert, Index and Tables.
4. If necessary, choose the Table of Contents tab.
5. Under Formats, choose a style for your table of contents. (Check under Preview to see how it will look.)
6. Click on OK or press ENTER.

Generates a table of contents and inserts it into the designated spot in your document. For this technique to work, the headings in your document must be formatted with Word's built-in heading styles. See OUTLINING for details on an easy way to apply heading styles.

If your document changes, you may need to update the table of contents. (The table of contents is actually a field; see FIELDS.) To do so, place the insertion point anywhere in the table of contents and press F9. Then either update page numbers only, or update the entire table of contents (choose this option if you've added any new headings).

TABLE OF FIGURES

1. If necessary, apply captions to any figures, tables, or drawings in your table (see CAPTIONS).
2. Place the insertion point where you want the table of figures to appear.
3. Choose Insert, Index and Tables.
4. If necessary, choose the Table of Figures tab.
5. Under Caption Label, choose which type of captions you want to generate a list of.
6. Under Formats, choose a style for your table of figures. (Check under Preview to see how it will look.)
7. Click on OK or press ENTER.

Generates a table of figures (or drawings, tables, or graphs) and places it in your document at the insertion point. For this technique to work, you must have inserted captions using the caption feature.

If your document changes, you may need to update the table of figures. (The table of figures is actually a field; see FIELDS.) To do so, place the insertion point anywhere in the table of figures and press F9. Then either update page numbers only, or update the entire table of figures (choose this option if you've added any new figures).

TABLES

You can use Word's table feature to enter data in any sort of tabular arrangement, to create forms, and in general to bring order to your documents. A *table* is a series of rows and columns; each row and column intersection is called a *cell*. Once you've created a table, you can enter text into individual cells much as you enter text in the normal editing screen. Text will wrap within the cell you enter it in, expanding the cell as needed. Note that you can also sort the contents of tables (see SORTING TEXT).

Creating Tables

1. Place the insertion point where you want to create a table.
2. Choose Table, Insert Table.
3. Choose how many rows and columns to include in your table.
4. Click on OK or press ENTER.

Mouse Shortcut:

 Click on the Insert Table button; then drag across grid to select number of columns and rows

Inserts a blank table of the specified number of columns and rows. Choose AutoFormat in the Insert Table dialog box to gain access to the table AutoFormat feature, which is described in a moment. Or, click on the Wizard button to activate the table wizard (see WIZARDS).

Moving the Insertion Point in a Table

You must move the insertion point to the right cell before entering data in a table. If you're using a mouse, just click in the desired cell to place the insertion point within it. Using the keyboard requires some special techniques.

Keyboard Shortcuts:

TAB	Moves insertion point to next cell (or adds a new row if insertion point is in lower-right cell of the table); also selects the cell's data if it contains any
SHIFT+TAB	Moves insertion point to previous cell; also selects the cell's data if it contains any
UP ARROW	Moves insertion point to previous row
DOWN ARROW	Moves insertion point to next row
LEFT ARROW	Moves insertion point to previous character or previous row
RIGHT ARROW	Moves insertion point to next character or next row
ALT+HOME	Moves insertion point to first cell in row
ALT+END	Moves insertion point to last cell in row
ALT+PGUP	Moves insertion point to first cell in column
ALT+PGDN	Moves insertion point to last cell in column

Selecting in Tables

You must select table cells, columns, or rows before performing actions that affect them. You can make selections using either the keyboard or the mouse.

In the Table menu, choose Select Row to select the row containing the insertion point; choose Select Column to select the column containing the insertion point; or choose Select Table to select the entire table.

Keyboard Shortcuts:

ALT+5 (numeric keypad with NUM LOCK off)	Selects entire table
TAB	Selects next cell (if it contains data)
SHIFT+TAB	Selects previous cell (if it contains data)
SHIFT+arrow keys	Selects multiple cells in the direction of the arrow

Mouse Shortcuts:

Click in cell's selection bar in left edge of cell (mouse pointer changes to right-pointing arrow)	Selects current cell
Click in selection bar to left of row	Selects current row

Click at top of column (cell pointer changes to downward-pointing arrow)	Selects current column
Drag	Selects multiple cells, columns, or rows

Deleting Cells, Columns, or Rows

To delete columns or rows:

1. Select the columns or rows you want to delete.
2. Choose Table, and then choose Delete Columns or Delete Rows.

To delete cells:

1. Select the cells you want to delete.
2. Choose Table, Delete Cells.
3. Choose whether to delete entire columns or rows, or whether to move cells to the left or up to fill in the gaps left by the deleted cells.

Enables you to delete table rows, columns, or cells when they are no longer needed. Do this when you want to alter the structure of the table. To remove data from the table—without actually removing table cells—you can select the cells containing that data and press DEL.

Gridlines

1. Choose Table, Gridlines.

Turns on or off *gridlines*—nonprinting lines that show the location of table cells. If you insert a table and see nothing on the screen, gridlines are off. To insert printing lines between table cells, use the border feature (see BORDERS) or the AutoFormat feature for tables, which is covered in a moment.

Inserting Cells, Columns, or Rows

To insert table rows or columns:

1. Select the row(s) or column(s) below which or to the right of which to insert new rows or columns. If you want to insert a single row or column, select a single row or column; if you want to insert two rows or columns, select two; and so on.
2. Choose Table, and then choose either Insert Rows or Insert Columns.

Inserts rows above the selected rows; inserts columns to the left of the selected columns. You can also add a row at the end of your table just by moving the insertion point to the lower-right cell in the table and pressing TAB.

To insert cells into a table:

1. Select one or more cells. (To insert one cell, select one cell; to insert two, select two; and so on.)

2. Choose Table, Insert Cells.

3. Choose whether to insert entire columns or rows, or whether to move cells to the right or down in order to insert the new cells to their left or above them.

4. Click on OK or press ENTER.

Mouse Shortcut:

 Inserts rows or columns, if rows or columns are selected; insert new cells, if cells are selected

Merging and Splitting Cells

To merge two or more cells:

1. Select the cells you want to combine.

2. Choose Table, Merge Cells.

To split cells:

1. Select the cells to be split.

2. Choose Table, Split Cells.

3. Either accept the suggested number of columns, or choose a new number.

4. Click on OK or press ENTER.

Lets you combine two or more cells to create a larger cell, or divide cells by splitting them. If you select multiple cells to be split, each cell (rather than all the cells combined) will be split into the indicated number of columns. (If you select three cells and choose 2 as the number of columns, the end result will be 6 columns, not 2 columns.) If there's data in cells that you merge, the data from each individual cell becomes a paragraph in the new, larger cell.

Modifying Row Height and Column Width

To change column widths:

1. Select the columns to be affected.

2. Choose T<u>a</u>ble, Cell Height and <u>W</u>idth.

3. Choose a new width for the selected columns; if you like, also change the <u>S</u>pace Between Columns setting to reserve more white space between columns.

4. Choose <u>P</u>revious Column or <u>N</u>ext Column to adjust the width of other columns in the table.

5. Click on OK or press ENTER.

Mouse Shortcuts:

Drag on a column boundary	Widens or narrows column to left of boundary, proportionally changing size of columns to right but not changing size of table as a whole
SHIFT+drag on a column boundary	Widens or narrows column to left of boundary, changing size of column just to its right but not affecting other columns and not altering width of table as a whole
CTRL+drag on a column boundary	Widens or narrows column to left of boundary, changing size of all columns to the right so that they're equal but not altering width of table as a whole
CTRL+SHIFT+drag on a column boundary	Widens or narrows column to left without affecting any other columns; changes the width of the table as a whole

Enables you to adjust the width of any or all columns in your table. Increasing the <u>S</u>pace Between Columns setting places the cell's contents farther from the cell boundary, adding more space between the contents of cells within the same row. You can also use Word's AutoFit feature to adjust column widths automatically. Just select the table to be affected, choose T<u>a</u>ble, Cell Height and <u>W</u>idth, choose <u>C</u>olumn, and then choose <u>A</u>utoFit. Word adjusts the columns to more closely fit the data they contain.

To change row heights:

1. Select the rows to be affected.

2. Choose T<u>a</u>ble, Cell Height and <u>W</u>idth.

3. Under H<u>e</u>ight of Rows, choose Auto to have Word adjust rows automatically to fit their contents; choose At Least and then specify a minimum height that Word

won't go below but may go above; or choose Exactly and then specify an exact row height that will not vary.

4. If you want, choose Next Row or Previous Row to adjust the height of other rows in your table.

5. Click on OK or press ENTER.

Allows you to specify the row height for any or all rows in your table. You can deselect the Allow Row to Break Across Pages check box to prevent individual rows from appearing on two different pages.

Table AutoFormat

1. Place the insertion point within the table to be formatted.

2. Choose Table, Table AutoFormat.

3. Choose the desired table design under Formats.

4. If you like, alter the predefined style you just picked out by making selections under Apply Special Formats To and Formats to Apply.

5. Click on OK or press ENTER.

Lets you quickly format your tables using a number of table designs provided with Word. You can make certain modifications to these prefabricated table designs by making selections in the Table AutoFormat dialog box. If you want more control over the appearance of your tables, you can create table designs of your own using the borders and shading features. (See BORDERS and SHADING.)

TABS

To set custom tab stops with the mouse:

1. Select the paragraphs to be affected.

2. Click on the Tab Alignment button at the left end of the horizontal ruler until it resembles the desired tab stop style—see below. (It looks like an "L" by default.)

3. Click in the desired spot on the horizontal ruler to insert a tab stop.

To set custom tab stops with the keyboard:

1. Choose the paragraphs to be affected.

2. Choose F<u>o</u>rmat, <u>T</u>abs.

3. Enter a tab stop position, select an alignment for it, and choose whether to include a leader.

4. Click on the <u>S</u>et button to establish the new tab.

5. Repeat steps 3 and 4 for all tab stops you want to set.

6. Click on OK or press ENTER.

Mouse Shortcuts:

 Enables you to create a left-aligned tab stop

 Enables you to create a right-aligned tab stop

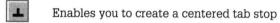 Enables you to create a centered tab stop

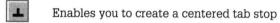 Enables you to create a decimal tab stop

Establishes the designated kind of custom tab stops in the locations you specify. If you set tabs with the F<u>o</u>rmat menu, you can alter the default tab stops. *Custom tabs* are tabs that you set in specified locations and that apply to the selected paragraphs only. *Default tabs,* in contrast, can only be set at specified intervals, affect the entire document, and show up only as very small tick marks at the bottom of the horizontal ruler. Setting a custom tab stop removes all the default tab stops to its left.

When using the Tabs dialog box, you can introduce tab stop leaders to fill in the blank areas between tab stops.

To clear custom tab stops with the mouse:

1. Select the paragraphs to be affected.

2. Drag the desired tabs stops off of the ruler.

3. Repeat steps 1 and 2 to remove as many tabs stops as needed.

To clear custom tab stops with the keyboard:

1. Select the paragraphs to be affected.

2. Choose F<u>o</u>rmat, <u>T</u>abs.

3. Select a tab under <u>T</u>ab Stop Position.

4. Click on the Cl<u>e</u>ar button, or select Clear <u>A</u>ll to remove all custom tab stops from the selected paragraphs.

5. Click on OK or press ENTER.

Removes the selected custom tab stops or all custom tab stops in the designated paragraphs. You can select Clear <u>A</u>ll to revert to the usual tab stops at half-inch intervals.

To change the default tab stops:

1. Choose F<u>o</u>rmat, <u>T</u>abs.
2. Enter the value you want between default tab stops under De<u>f</u>ault Tab Stops.
3. Click on OK or press ENTER.

Changes the default tab stops that are in effect for the entire document. For example, you could do this if you wanted tab stops every inch (instead of every half inch) throughout your document.

TEMPLATES

A *template* is a ready-made document design. Templates can include text, formatting, and graphics. They can also contain macros; AutoText entries; styles; and customized toolbars, menus, and shortcut keys. Word comes with a number of templates upon which you can base your documents. (In fact, all documents are based upon a template; the Normal template, Word's standard template, is used to create documents by default.) In addition, you can modify Word's templates or create templates of your own. If you frequently create similar documents, templates can greatly speed up your work.

Creating new documents based upon templates is covered under NEW FILE. Also see WIZARDS, Word's new feature for guiding you through document creation. The ORGANIZER section explains how to move AutoText entries, macros, styles, and toolbars between templates.

Creating Templates

To create a template based upon an existing template:

1. Choose <u>F</u>ile, <u>O</u>pen.
2. Under List Files of <u>T</u>ype, choose Document Templates.
3. If necessary, select WINWORD\TEMPLATE under <u>D</u>irectories (this directory is the repository of Word's templates).
4. Choose a template name under File <u>N</u>ame.

5. Click on OK or press ENTER to open the template.

6. Choose File, Save As and enter a different file name to save a copy of the template under a new name (this keeps the original template intact). Don't enter an extension; in the TEMPLATE directory, Word automatically assigns the .DOT extension.

7. Make the desired changes to the template. You can delete any elements you don't want; insert text or graphics; set margins and other page layout attributes; modify and create styles; create macros and AutoText entries; and customize menus, toolbars, and shortcut keys.

8. Choose File, Save.

Creates a new template that you can use to create documents in the future. Choose the existing template that most nearly matches the desired end results; this will require fewer modifications on your part. To see which styles are available with what templates, use the Style Gallery (see STYLES).

You can also modify an existing template—instead of creating a new one—by following the preceding steps but saving the template under the same name rather than a different name (use File, Save).

THESAURUS

1. Select the word for which you want to look up alternatives.

2. Choose Tools, Thesaurus.

3. To replace the word, choose a word under Replace with Synonym and then choose Replace.

4. To look up additional synonyms, select a new word under Meanings to see a new list under Replace with Synonym, or select a word under Replace with Synonym and choose Look Up.

5. If necessary, choose the Cancel button to return to your document.

Keyboard Shortcut:

SHIFT+F7   Opens the Thesaurus dialog box and looks up the selected word

Helps you look up alternatives for the selected word. When a word is selected under Meanings, any synonyms show up under Replace with Synonyms. You may also be able to choose Antonyms under Meanings to look up antonyms of the word listed under Looked Up. You can choose the Previous button to return to words that you've already looked up, and you can pull down the Looked Up drop-down list box and choose from recent word selections to look them up again.

TOOLBARS

1. Choose View, Toolbars.
2. Select the check boxes for the toolbars that you want to display, or deselect the check boxes for toolbars to hide.

Hides or displays the selected toolbars. There are also specialty toolbars that only appear when you're performing a specific task—such as creating an outline or recording a macro. These appear and disappear as needed. When you position the mouse pointer over a toolbar button, its name is displayed right below and a brief description appears in the lower-left corner of the screen. To turn off the display of button names, deselect Show ToolTips in the Toolbars dialog box. You can also turn off color for buttons, and can display larger buttons if you like.

You can create a new toolbar by clicking on the New button in the Toolbars dialog box, entering a toolbar name, choosing which templates you want the toolbar to be available in, and choosing OK. Then add buttons to the toolbar as described under CUSTOMIZE. If you create a new toolbar that you decide not to keep, just highlight its name in the Toolbars dialog box and choose the Delete button. Also see ORGANIZER for details on deleting, copying, and renaming toolbars. The Reset button in the Toolbars dialog box reverses any changes you've made to the toolbars supplied with Word.

Some toolbars (such as the Standard toolbar right beneath the menu bar) are "anchored" at the edge of the editing screen. Others "float" within the editing screen. To move an anchored toolbar so that it floats on the editing screen, place the mouse pointer between its buttons and drag, or else hold down the SHIFT key while double-clicking a blank area on the toolbar. Once a toolbar is floating, you can reposition it by dragging on its title bar. In addition, you can return a floating toolbar to its original location by double-clicking on its title bar. You can even resize floating toolbars by dragging on their borders.

UNDERLINING

1. Choose the text to be affected.
2. Choose Format, Font.
3. If necessary, choose the Font tab.
4. Pull down the Underline drop-down list box and choose the type of underlining you want.
5. Click on OK or press ENTER.

Keyboard Shortcuts:

CTRL+U	Applies (or removes) single underlining to all selected words and spaces
CTRL+SHIFT+W	Applies (or removes) single underlining to all selected words, but does not underline spaces
CTRL+SHIFT+D	Applies (or removes) double underlining to all selected words and spaces

Mouse Shortcuts:

    Underlines the selected text with single underlining, or removes such underlining if it already exists

Underlines the selected text. You can remove underlining by selecting the text, following the preceding steps, and choosing [none] from the Underline drop-down list box. You can also underline text as you type by choosing the Underline button or using the Format, Font command, typing the desired text, and then deselecting the Underline button or setting underlining to [none].

UNDO

1. Choose Edit, Undo.

Keyboard Shortcut:

CTRL+Z	Reverses one or more of the previous operations

Mouse Shortcut:

    Reverses one or more of the previous operations

Lets you reverse the effects of one or more previous operations. The complete command name changes depending on the operation being undone—it might be something like Undo Typing or Undo Bold, for example.

You can reverse several operations, not just the most recent one. For example, if you typed something and then applied boldfacing, you could undo both the boldfacing and the typing, in that order, by choosing the Undo command from the Edit menu twice. You can also select the Undo button repeatedly, or click on the downward-pointing arrow to its right and choose one or more actions to undo from the list that appears. If you change your mind after undoing an operation, you can always redo it; you can even reverse the effects of multiple undo operations (see REDO).

WINDOWS

Generally, when you work in Word, you'll just have a single document—in a single window—displayed on your screen. However, Word for Windows provides a number of options for displaying and manipulating windows, both so you can view several documents at once and so you can get various views of the same document. (Also see "Working with Multiple Documents" under "General Procedures.")

Activating an Open Document

1. Open the Window menu, and then choose the name of the document you want to activate.

Keyboard Shortcut:
CTRL+F6   Activates the next open window

Activates one of the open windows. You can have many open windows but can only work within one window at a time; this is called the *active window*. For details on opening documents, see OPENING FILES and "Opening and Closing Files" under "General Procedures."

If a single document is displayed, activating a new window displaces the display of the original document, replacing it with the new one. This is not true if you have several documents displayed, as described next.

Arranging All Open Windows

1. Choose Window, Arrange All.

Displays all open documents in a nonoverlapping fashion
(only has an effect if you have more than one document
open). This lets you see and work with all your open
documents, but the more documents you have open, the
smaller their windows.

Even when several windows are displayed at once, only
one of them can be active. To change the active window,
click within the window you want to activate or use the
Window menu. This highlights the window's title bar and
places the insertion point within it, but does not change
the arrangement of windows on the screen. If you want
to see only the document you just activated, click on its
Maximize button (the upward-pointing triangle in its
upper-right corner). For further details on changing the
size of windows, consult your Windows documentation .

Opening a New Window

1. Choose Window, New Window.

Opens a new window containing the exact same contents
as the active window. You can use this command in
combination with Window, Arrange All to view different
areas of the same document at the same time, or to view
a single document in different views. The two open
windows are considered a single document, and changes
in one show up in the other. In other words, don't confuse
opening a new window containing the same document
with opening a new document, as described under NEW
FILE. Also see "Splitting Windows."

Splitting Windows

1. Choose Window, Split.
2. Press the arrow keys to move the split marker, and
   press ENTER when it's located where you want to insert
   the split.

Mouse Shortcut:

Drag or double-click on the split box (the black horizontal bar at the top of the vertical scroll bar)	Divides the active document into two separate panes, or returns it to a single pane

Enables you to split your document into two *panes*—that is, two separate areas that can show different portions of the same document. This lets you view different areas of a long document at the same time. Note that only one copy of the document is open, and any changes you make in one pane show up in the other pane.

To view two different documents at once—instead of just getting two views of the same document—see "Arranging All Open Windows." To remove the split and just see a single window pane, either issue the Window, Remove Split command, drag the split box back up to the top of the screen, or double-click on the split box.

WIZARDS

1. Choose File, New.
2. Under Template, select the desired wizard.
3. Make sure Document is selected under New and click on OK or press ENTER.
4. Respond to the wizard's prompts about how you want your document constructed.
5. If applicable, choose Next to continue, or Back to go back to the previous step, and continue to make selections.
6. When you're done, choose Finish to close the wizard and get into the document you've just created.

Initiates a *wizard*, which guides you through the process of creating a specific type of document. The wizard displays dialog boxes requesting your input in order to determine your document's basic layout, formatting, and, in some cases, content. When you're done, you may need to complete your newly created document by adding any needed text or graphics. Also see NEW FILE.

Word provides wizards for everything from letters to memos to tables to newsletters. In certain cases, you can even use or modify prewritten letters that are included with Word. With wizards, Word has come about as close as possible to having documents generate themselves.

WORD COUNT

1. Choose Tools, Word Count.
2. In the Word Count dialog box, select the Include Footnotes and Endnotes check box to have these items included in the count.
3. Click on OK or press ENTER to return to your document when you're done viewing the display.

Counts the number of pages, words, characters, paragraphs, and lines in the active document. Note that hidden text is not included in the count unless it is displayed. (See HIDDEN TEXT.)

ZOOM

1. Choose View, Zoom.
2. Under Zoom To, choose by how much to enlarge or reduce the display.
3. Click on OK or press ENTER.

Mouse Shortcut:

Pull down this Zoom Control box and choose the desired zoom percentage or zoom setting

Enables you to enlarge the displayed document—viewing less of it in greater detail—or to reduce the display so you can get an overview. Aside from choosing a display percentage, you can choose Page Width to display your document so that it fits between the left and right margins; choose Whole Page to display an entire page on the screen (Page Layout view or Print Preview only); and choose Two Pages (in the Zoom Control box) or Many Pages to view two or more pages (Page Layout or Print Preview).

Index

M

T